THE POWER OF A DREAM

THE POWER OF A DREAM

Peter Legge
with
Tashon Ziara

Eaglet Publishing

Eaglet Publishing
Peter Legge Management Co. Ltd.
4th Floor, 4180 Lougheed Highway
Burnaby, British Columbia, V5C 6A7, Canada
Tel. (604) 299-7311 Fax (604) 299-9188

Library and Archives Canada Cataloguing in Publication

Legge, Peter, 1942-
   The power of a dream: your dream is still possible / by
   Peter Legge; with Tashon Ziara.

ISBN 978-0-9781459-7-2

1. Success. 2. Self-actualization (Psychology). I. Ziara,
   Tashon II. Title.

BF637.S8L4534 2010   158.1   C2010-906274-4

Jacket design by Catherine Mullaly; cover photo by
Robert Harding/Getty Images; electronic imaging by
Berny Holzmann; Typeset by Ina Bowerbank;
Edited by Kim Mah
Printed and bound in Canada by Friesens Corporation

Dedicated to
My two granddaughters

Cate Grace
(Born January 21, 2009)

And to
Carys Emerson
(Born June 28, 2010)

"It is no small thing, when they, who are
so fresh from God, love us."
— Charles Dickens

Other Books by the Author

How to Soar With the Eagles
You Can If You Believe You Can
It Begins With a Dream
If Only I'd Said That
If Only I'd Said That: Volume II
If Only I'd Said That: Volume III
If Only I'd Said That: Volume IV
If Only I'd Said That: Volume V
Who Dares Wins
The Runway of Life
Make Your Life a Masterpiece
The Power of Tact
The Power to Soar Higher

Booklets

97 Tips on How to Do Business in Tough Times
97 Tips on Customer Service
97 Tips on How to Jumpstart Your Career

CD

The Runway of Life

DVD

Doing Business in Tough Times

TABLE OF CONTENTS

INTRODUCTION

As the Greek physician Hippocrates so famously stated, "Life is short."

Yes, life is indeed very short.

If we don't hit too many potholes along the way, living to 85 years of age is quite possible, but it still isn't as much time as you would imagine. When you break it down, that's a mere 4,420 weeks — doesn't seem quite as long now, does it?

Several years ago, my longtime friend and mentor, Joe Segal shared an illustration with me that he had drawn on a napkin while we were having lunch together at his favourite restaurant. Basically, he explained as he scribbled, it's a straight line that starts at whatever age you are right now and ends . . . well, that's the thing of it, we never know exactly where or when it's going to end. The only thing we can be sure of is that it *will* end! Joe calls that line the Runway of Life and the point he was making is that eventually, we all run out of runway.

How long do you think your runway of life is?

If you think your life will end at 85 years and you're 55 now, you've got 30 years left on your runway.

Take a moment to do the math for your own life.

Approaching 70 years of age, my guess is that my own runway has about 15 years or 780 weeks left. (Yikes!)

The big question is, what will you do with the time that you have?

In the weeks, months and years you have left, do you

have hopes, dreams, vision and purpose for your life?

If not, this book, *The Power of a Dream: Your Dream is Still Possible*, may help.

Recently, I spent a weekend in Kelowna, B.C., at the Mission Hill Family Estate winery being entertained by the Canadian Tenors and raising money for a little town in Swaziland, Africa. What brought these three together?

Three big dreams coming together for one inspiring purpose.

The first was Anthony von Mandl, O.B.C., who is the proprietor of Mission Hill. Intensity, infectious passion and an unwavering commitment to living life to its full potential define Anthony. He has dedicated his entire life's work to one audacious dream: to produce world-renowned wines in British Columbia's Okanagan Valley and showcase them at a landmark winery, one that would be a legacy for generations to come. His premium wine is called Oculus, which is Latin for vision. I believe that's also another word for dream. During the past 25 years, Anthony has built his dream, a world-class winery located in the heart of the Okanagan Valley that produces award-winning wines and sells over a quarter-million cases of wine each year.

The second dream involves four young Canadian men, who have been crisscrossing the globe, thrilling millions of music lovers with their magnificent voices and wonderful sense of humour. They've entertained audiences in over 100 cities, including locations in South Africa, Holland, Ireland, England, the United States, Asia and, of course, Canada. From humble beginnings, today they are known as the Canadian Tenors and are internationally famous for their music and generosity of spirit.

The third part of the story relates to a little village in Swaziland called Bulembu. In 2001, the U.K. mining company that had built and operated Bulembu for more than 60 years closed its doors and walked away. With no jobs for the inhabitants, the town was soon abandoned. Located in a country that continues to be ravaged by the A.I.D.S. pandemic, the result was an orphan crisis for Bulembu. Enter Volker Wagner, a B.C. man whose dream after visiting Bulembu in 2004, was to buy the town and apply his mind, body, soul and spirit to restoring the lives and the heart of this little community — a pretty big dream to be sure.

On that recent weekend in mid-September, all three groups came together for this one big dream and raised $1.25 million in a single evening for the little village of Bulembu. An inspiring example of the power of a dream!

Samuel Johnson once said, "It is necessary to hope." He went on to say, "Hope itself is happiness and its frustrations, however frequent, are less dreadful than its extinction."

We hope . . . for the future, as yet unknown.

We hope . . . for a successful career.

We hope . . . for happiness, fulfillment and a meaningful life.

We hope . . . to devote our talents for the good and to use them to their fullest.

When we apply substance to our hopes — take action and put some meat on the bones — they turn into dreams and only then are we in a position to bring them to life.

My dream for this book is that it will encourage and inspire you to figure out what your dreams are and to get moving on them, for the time left on our runway grows ever shorter. And the last thing we want, I believe, is to be at the end of our runway asking the question, why didn't I act on that dream? Why didn't I walk through the doors that opened for me? Why didn't I seize the opportunities that presented themselves? Because as we close our eyes and take our last breath, it will be too late.

So, get moving today. You have within you enormous resources, untapped talents and abilities, intelligence and opportunities that have been denied to many. Seize today — *carpe diem*!

The Power of a Dream can change lives, it can change families, organizations of all sizes, even villages in Africa. But most importantly, the Power of a Dream can change YOU. Your dream is still possible.

Peter Legge
September 2010

CHAPTER 1

WHAT ARE YOU DOING FOR THE REST OF YOUR LIFE?

People approach me all the time and tell me, "I want to do something else with my life. I have a dream, how do I go about making it happen?" My answer to the question is always this, "What are you prepared to sacrifice for your dream and what are you willing to do to make it happen?"

If you want to be the next Bill Gates, are you willing to start a business in your garage and work as long and as diligently as he did to make his dream come true? Likewise, if you dream of being a superstar goalie in the NHL like Roberto Luongo, are you ready to put in the years and years of practice to hone your skills and work your way up from the bottom? Lots of people say they'd like to be as rich as British Columbian billionaire Jimmy Pattison, but how many are willing to put in the time, effort, energy and commitment that Jimmy does to have what he has?

One day I was listening to a concert pianist play as he prepared for a performance. "I would give my life to play like you do," I told him. "I did give my life to do this," was his reply.

What are you willing to give your life for?

We all have dreams. The only difference between those

who achieve their dreams and those who don't is the action they do or don't take.

I have had many dreams in my lifetime. As readers of my 2009 book *The Power to Soar Higher* will know, one of my most recent dreams involved the Olympics. In 2003, International Olympic Committee chairman Jacques Rogge announced that the city of Vancouver would host the 2010 Olympic and Paralympic Winter Games. In December 2007, I received a letter from John Furlong, head of the Vancouver Organizing Committee, inviting me to be an Olympic ambassador.

Shortly after receiving the letter, I said to myself, "There really is nothing bigger than the Olympics. This is a great opportunity and I should find some way to be involved and make the most of what would surely be a once-in-a-lifetime experience taking place right in my own backyard." After thinking about it for awhile, an idea came to me. 'I've got a pretty good voice,' I thought. 'Maybe I could be emcee for the opening and closing ceremonies.'

I talked to fellow governor of the Vancouver Board of Trade, Rick Turner, who was also a director of the Vancouver Organizing Committee, and he said, "Go for it, Peter." So I did.

I spoke with John Furlong and let him know of my interest and about a year later, I got an email from Rick Turner asking me if I was, or could be, bilingual in both of Canada's official languages (French and English) in time for the Olympics. Even though I knew right then and there that there was no realistic chance of my becoming bilingual in such a short time, I didn't give up. Instead, I thought,

'Who do I know that is bilingual?' Then it dawned on me. Not only had my daughter Rebecca completed her grade-school education in a French immersion program, she also attended university in Nice, France. If bilingualism were required, we would make the perfect father-daughter team.

The challenge now was to convince John Furlong that I was the man for the job. I realized that I would have to do something extraordinary. Deciding that a professional demo was the way to go, I hired the local Knowledge Network television studio with all of their staff for a few hours and produced a demo video for the opening ceremonies. When I presented the demo to John, he was both surprised and impressed. "I've never seen someone go to so much trouble for a job that doesn't pay any money," he told me.

By the time I had produced my demo, the Vancouver Organizing Committee had already engaged David Atkins from Australia to produce the opening and closing ceremonies. Speaking with David, he told me that it was unlikely that I would have a chance at being emcee, as this was an off-camera job and one that was generally decided by the television network with the rights to broadcast the Games.

"We need to find you something else to do," he told me, much to my delight.

Many emails and almost two years later (remember, it takes at least 10 tries to make a sale and most people give up after the third try), it was decided that I would give a six-minute motivational address at the very first Victory Ceremony (the ceremony where they hand out the medals to athletes) to be held at B.C. Place Stadium during the Olympics. Although it wasn't exactly my dream as I had originally imagined it, I was very proud to be the only motivational speaker — in the entire world — to be invited to speak at the Olympics.

Life doesn't turn out exactly how we expect it to, I never did get to emcee the opening or closing ceremonies, but I did end up playing a role in the Olympics and making some wonderful memories, all because I took action and set my dream in motion.

What about your dreams? Are you stuck on autopilot? It happens to many people after they leave school and find a job. Too many end up sleepwalking through life, doing what they have to do to get by, but not really living and not really enjoying the journey.

Have you thought about your own situation and asked, "Is this the life I want? Am I doing what I was meant to do? Am I excited about what the future holds?" If you don't know or you aren't getting a deep sense of fulfillment from whatever you're presently focused on, maybe it's time to ask some more questions and spend some time considering your options. But don't be frustrated if the answers don't come immediately. Very few people are actually born knowing exactly what they want from life, and for most of us, our dreams change as we grow and change. It can take time and exploration to figure out what gets you excited, what inspires you, what motivates you and what talents you have that you can share with the world. It's never too late to start living your dream, and many of the stories in this book are about people who have decided to pursue a different dream in their 50s, 60s or even later.

Sometimes it takes a traumatic event like being fired from a job to wake us up to opportunity or make us realize that we've somehow wandered down a path that isn't taking us where we want to go. There's a scene in the movie *Up in the Air*, where the main character, Ryan Bingham (played by George Clooney), is doing an exit interview with one of the employees he has just fired. That's what his character does in the movie — he fires people for a living. When corporations need to downsize quickly but don't have the courage to drop the axe themselves, he flies in and breaks the news to the people being fired. In the scene, Ryan is talking to Bob, who is in his 50s: "Your resumé says you minored in French Culinary Arts. Most students work the fryer at KFC. You bussed tables at Il Picatorre to support yourself. Then you got out of college and started working here [he was being fired from an office job in a big company where he had clearly worked for decades]. How much did they pay you to give up on your dreams?"

"Twenty-seven thousand a year," replies Bob.

"At what point were you going to stop and go back to what made you happy?" asks Bingham. "I see guys who work at the same company for their entire life, guys exactly like you. They clock in, they clock out and they never have a moment of happiness. You have an opportunity . . . this is a rebirth. If not for you, do it for your children."

At what point in *your* life are you going to decide to go after what truly makes you happy?

Dream big dreams
If you've read my book, *The Runway of Life*, you'll remember how we calculated just how much time each of us can expect to have to accomplish all of the things we want to do. If we're lucky, each of us will live for about 4,420 weeks. When you think about how quickly a week goes by, it seems like a lot less than 85 years. When we break it down, say into how many more birthdays we can hope to share with the ones we love, or how many more summers we will have to enjoy, we realize that time is short and it slips by much quicker than we imagined, so it is important to make the most of every day, every hour and even every minute. Therefore, my advice to you is if you are planning to live life to the fullest and have the opportunity to explore all of those inviting corners, you have to hustle. You have to dream big dreams and live them.

Don't be a prisoner to your potential
As I mentioned in my book *The Power to Soar Higher*, two summers ago, my wife Kay and I had a unique opportunity to cruise the Mediterranean on a small cruise ship called *The Seabourn Legend*. There were only 196 passengers, which made for an intimate and relaxing voyage.

At one of the ports of call along the way, we took a day trip to see the city of Florence, Italy. Our first tourist stop of the day was to the museum Galleria dell'Accademia where we got a first-hand look at the 13-and-a-half-foot-tall sculpture of David by Michelangelo. It took him three years to finish this colossus.

As you walk slowly towards "The David," you are

reminded that Michelangelo worked on 45 sculptures in his lifetime and only completed 14 of them (if each completed work took three years, that would be 42 years of work). David and Moses are probably the most famous of those that he did complete. As you approach "The David," you pass by unfinished statues called *The Prisoners, Atlantis, The Young Slave, The Beardless Slave* and *The Awakening Slave*. These are the unfinished works and unfulfilled potential of a true genius.

It's been said by some people that the average person generally develops only about two per cent of his or her potential over a lifetime, although others estimate that we use as much as 10 per cent of our potential. I imagine if you were to use 25 per cent of your potential, you would be called a genius like Michelangelo.

Given these estimates, what's truly astonishing is the amount of potential we will never use. Even if we double the higher number of 10 per cent to 20 per cent, that still leaves five per cent of our potential untapped. Wow! What an opportunity we have to better ourselves.

The best part is that it doesn't take much to start using more of our potential. As we look around our workplace, our community and even our home life, we can clearly see our own "blocks of stone" that, as yet, have not been developed in order to unlock our hidden potential.

How best to start? This book is full of ideas and stories about people who are pursuing their own dreams — dreams that come in all shapes and sizes. My purpose in sharing these stories is to demonstrate that every one of us has the potential to fulfill our dreams, but it takes action and commitment to get there. It is my hope that you will find inspiration from the many people in this book, people like my friend and business associate, Mel Zajac.

In two separate tragic accidents, Mel lost both of his sons. Following a period of grieving, he decided to channel his energy and love for his sons into something healthy to help other kids. He had a dream to create an amazing place where children with disabilities or serious health concerns could go to have fun and feel like normal kids for a change. To fulfill his dream, together with his wife, he established the Mel Jr. and Marty Zajac Foundation and the Zajac Ranch for Children in Maple Ridge, B.C. It's difficult to gauge the impact that Mel's dream has had on kids who attend the ranch's programs each summer, but it is obvious that it has helped hundreds of kids with disabilities to do things that otherwise seemed impossible. Two years ago, Mel Zajac was awarded the Order of Canada for his philanthropy and he continues to live his dream.

So, what are you doing for the rest of your life?

It takes a bit of courage to live your dreams, but I know you've got what it takes and you do too! If you don't believe me, just think of all the times you have discovered that you actually can achieve what you set out to do. Yet remember how nervous you were going into that seemingly impossible challenge? The halting steps? But you did it, you believed in yourself and you went ahead anyway. Afterwards, did you say to yourself, "Hey, that wasn't so difficult, what's next?" or did you settle back into your comfortable niche once again? Most dreams don't happen on their own; it takes consistent effort to make them a reality.

—ɷ—

One of my favourite authors is John Maxwell from Atlanta, Georgia. In the introduction to his book, *Put Your Dream to the Test*, he asks the following questions:

What is your dream? Will you achieve it in your lifetime? I'm certain that you desire to do it. What odds would you give yourself?
    One in five?
    One in a hundred?
    One in a million?
    How can you tell what your chances are or whether your dream will always remain exactly that, a dream?
    Most people have no idea how to achieve their dreams.
    Many people pursue things that they call dreams.
    Daydreams.
    Pie-in-the-sky dreams.
    Bad dreams.
    Idealistic dreams.
    Career-only dreams.
    Destination dreams.
    Material dreams.

Research shows that approximately 95 per cent of us have never written out our goals (dreams) for our lives. But, of the five per cent who have, 95 per cent of them have achieved their dreams/goals. In 1953 at Yale University, three per cent of the graduating class had specific, written goals for their lives. In 1975, researchers found that the three per cent who had written down their goals accomplished more than the other 97 per cent put together.

Every millionaire or billionaire I've ever talked to tells me that the biggest secret to his or her success has been to dream big dreams, plan for the long term and keep moving forward. These people didn't get where they are by taking a leisurely bus ride up the hill, they decided early on that they were going to the very top of the mountain and they began to chart a course that would get them there.

Microsoft billionaire Bill Gates, a man whom we all watch and listen to with great interest, says that his success in business has largely been the result of his ability to focus on long-term goals and ignore short-term distractions. Despite all of his success, he continues to dream big dreams about developments within his own industry and he creates the opportunities — bringing together the right people and the right technology — that can make them happen.

"When change is inevitable," says Mr. Gates, "you must spot it, embrace it and find ways to make it work for you." That's first-hand advice from someone who dreams big dreams and has literally changed the world as a result.

Of course, it can be intimidating to compare our lives to that of someone like Bill Gates. You might say to yourself that he was the right person in the right place at the right time; that he got the breaks; that no one will ever again succeed quite like he has succeeded. When comparing bank accounts, that may well be. But while Mr. Gates may have a special niche in the business world, there is also a special niche in the world for you — you just have to find it.

When I talk of dreaming, I'm not talking about day-dreaming. Dreaming involves doing. You dream big and you start to make it come true. You write it down and share it with your spouse or a close friend. You begin to plot your course and look for likeminded people who can help you along the way, you breathe some life into it, keep fanning the flames that will make it burn brighter and remember that everything you do, say or think counts.

I myself have dreamed big dreams and many of them have come true as a result. And I keep dreaming, reaching out a little more, taking calculated risks, believing that if I've climbed this far — and the view has been fantastic — then I can certainly continue to climb higher and higher.

We humans thrive on achievement and the bigger we dream, the more we achieve. Billionaire Jimmy Pattison, whom I mentioned at the beginning of this chapter, once told me that those men and women who dare to dream big dreams are the only ones who have the ability to achieve those dreams.

Canadian actor and comic Jim Carrey is a case in point. Early in his career, he was a stand-up comic playing the comedy club circuit in North America but he dreamed of international stardom. Following his acclaimed success in the movies *Ace Ventura: Pet Detective*, *The Mask* and *Batman Forever*, he was interviewed on a Barbara Walters television special. In this now-legendary interview, he talked about his struggle to make it at the beginning of his career, the long, lonely nights on the road and how six or seven years previously he had written a cheque to himself for $10 million and dated it October 1995. He kept this huge dream in his wallet, looking at it every day. In 1995, Jim Carrey signed a contract to star in the sequel to *Ace Ventura* for — you guessed it — $10 million. Shortly afterward, he received a record sum for a comedy actor when he was paid $20 million to star in the movie, *The Cable Guy*. Today, Carrey continues to dream big dreams and continually reinvent himself as an actor by exploring new territory.

Was it coincidence, fate or luck that Carrey was able to realize his dream — or the fact that he carried his dream around with him every single day to keep him focused and moving towards his goal?

"You become what you think about most of the time." It's a thought that has been attributed to many people, but I remember it coming from the late, great motivator Earl Nightingale. It's a truth that never loses its resonance.

Ralph Waldo Emerson, a man who spoke and wrote with eloquence about almost everything, said, "If the single man plant himself indomitably on his instincts, and there abide, the huge world will come round to him." I interpret that to mean that while it may take time and while we may have to struggle to find what we're looking for, if we stay focused on what we want to achieve, it will come to fruition.

Of course, in any hunt for treasure, it helps to have a map, the keys to the secret doors and the password to enter the hidden chamber . . . you can begin right now with Secret No. 1 (which, as I say elsewhere in this book, isn't really a secret): Identify your big dream. Dream it. Do it.

Are you ready to do it? Great! Let's get started.

SOMETHING TO THINK ABOUT

It's important to figure out what you want from your life so you don't waste the precious little time that you have.

"Every day, each of us makes a multitude of choices that will impact our lives . . . the quality of our choices will dictate whether we will struggle in frustration or live an extraordinary life — the life of our dreams."
— Debbie Ford, author of *The Right Questions*

CHAPTER 2

COULD FAILURE BE GOOD FOR YOU?

Most of us view failure as a bad thing — but is it really? What if, as we talked about in Chapter 1, a failure such as losing your job presents you with the opportunity to follow a lifelong dream? What if it wakes you up to the fact that you didn't really like that job anyway and had been marking time, not sure what to do about it and scared to take a leap of faith and make a change?

Even the most adventurous amongst us are afraid of change and even the most negative events in our lives can turn into something very positive if we look for the opportunity.

What are you afraid of?

Every one of us has fears, many of them totally irrational, but they terrify us nonetheless. Allow me to share what I'm afraid of:

- My wife Kay might leave me.
- One or more of my three children will get sick, be in a car accident or be seriously injured.
- Something might happen to one of my three grandchildren, Cate, Benjamin or Carys.
- I might lose my voice and be unable to do speaking engagements or host the Variety Telethon.

- My company might not survive a continued world-wide economic downturn.
- I might have to lay off some of my staff.
- I could lose my health, have another stroke or get cancer again.
- I might not have enough money to live on when I retire.
- I might not realize the completion of my dreams!

Looking at the list, you can see that I'm worried about many of the same things that you worry about. But the biggest concern for me is my dreams, as I still have some important ones that I would like to achieve. Coincidentally, my dreams are probably the one thing on the list that I have the greatest amount of control over.

I believe if you don't have dreams, you don't have anything. The humanitarian and former first lady of the United States, Eleanor Roosevelt, once said, "The future belongs to those who believe in the beauty of their dreams."

I also believe that most of us are far more afraid of failure than we need to be. Failure is a wonderful tool that acts like an alarm call, helping us realize when we need to make adjustments in our plan or ditch the plan altogether and make a new one.

In his book, *Better Than Good*, Zig Ziglar talks about all of the things that we can learn from failure. Following are some of the important lessons we can learn once we get our ego out of the way and realize that as long as we are willing to keep going and keep trying new things, we aren't failing, we're learning.

Five important things we can learn from our failures:

1. Failure teaches us to be flexible and make corrections when things aren't working the way we planned.
In the 1940s, a young Jewish boy chose to skip university in order to pursue his dream of becoming the next Benny Goodman. Going against his parents' advice, he began playing in a jazz band.

Unfortunately, his musical abilities weren't substantial enough to pay the bills and he soon realized that he was just another musician teetering on the brink of unemployment. However, unlike many of his fellow musicians, he was very good at managing the money he had, which meant that those periods of unemployment weren't nearly as devastating for him as they were for others.

Recognizing his talent for money management, his musical colleagues began to pay him to manage their finances as well. This led the young man to rethink his career goals and it also changed the course of his life.

That young man's name was Alan Greenspan and he went on to serve as long-time chairman of the United States Federal Reserve (1987-2006). His failure as a musician not only taught him resilience and self-reliance (important skills that we can all use in life), it also taught him that he had other, significant talents, to share with the world. Just like Mr. Greenspan, our failures can help us to discover how our interests and aptitudes can lead us to fulfill our destiny and purpose.

Sometimes, finding out what doesn't work is as important

as finding out what does — and there is no doubt that failure teaches us what doesn't work. When we fail, we eliminate at least one of the possibilities on our list and are free to pursue other ideas and options. In many ways, failure can actually be very cleansing. It gives us the ability to start anew with a modified or entirely new direction or outlook that has a new opportunity (and probability) for success. The moment we move on, we have a fresh chance to succeed (or fail) and the opportunity to apply what we have learned.

Of course, nobody likes to fail or miss the mark, but there is so much we can learn from each attempt we make, and every time we try again, it gets easier. Imagine inventor Thomas Edison in his workshop, trying to develop the light bulb. It took him 9,000 tries before he finally made one that worked. But with every attempt he made corrections that helped him to improve upon the next attempt and in doing so, he pushed himself that little bit closer to success. Like Edison, if we stay flexible and keep trying, we can literally fail our way to success.

2. Failure teaches us that we are never too smart to make a mistake.
Albert Einstein was clearly a brilliant man whose work contributed much to the advancement of science and our understanding of physics. But if you think that geniuses get it right every time, you'd be wrong. Einstein made plenty of mistakes, famous ones even, but that never stopped him from continuing to develop new theories and ideas about the universe.

In his book titled *Einstein's Mistakes: The Human Failings of Genius*, author Hans Ohanian talks about how scientists have identified serious flaws in four of the five papers that established Einstein's reputation in theoretical physics in 1905. Ohanian also points out Einstein's repeated failure to provide a valid proof for his most famous equation, $E = mc^2$, and talks about how, despite his repeated mistakes and in some cases, because of them, time after time Einstein came to correct conclusions and achieved theoretical breakthroughs that eluded other scientists — which goes a long way to explain why he remains an iconic scientist and household name so many decades later.

Imagine if Einstein had believed that his genius meant that he wasn't allowed to make mistakes, or worse, allowed his failures to stop him from continuing forward with the development of his theories. Like Einstein, we should allow our failures to act as the stepping stones that eventually lead us to success.

3. Failure teaches us that we can't always get what we want, but sometimes not getting what we want leads us to discover something even better.
Following the Second World War, Soichiro Honda applied for the position of engineer with the Toyota Motor Corporation but was turned down for the job. Unemployed, he started to make homemade scooters in his own small workshop and sell them to his friends and neighbours. As word spread and demand for his economical scooters grew, he decided to take the plunge and start his own company, Honda. Since then, the company has

grown to become the world's largest motorcycle manufacturer and one of the most profitable automakers — beating giants such as General Motors and Chrysler. With a global network of 437 subsidiaries, today Honda develops, manufactures and markets a wide variety of products ranging from small general-purpose engines and scooters to specialty sports cars.

In my own life, it took getting fired to finally motivate me to fulfill my dream of owning my own business. It was the summer of 1975 and I was the general sales manager of a radio station in British Columbia's Fraser Valley, which is just east of Vancouver. On a Thursday morning just before noon — we never seem to forget the little details of significant turning points in our lives — the station's president fired me.

A short memo to the staff said: "Peter Legge is no longer employed by this station. It will be business as usual."

Business as usual? Maybe for the station, but certainly not for me.

I'm not the first person or the last person ever to be fired. But for me it *was* the first time and I vowed right then that it would also be the last.

As with anyone who has ever been fired, I wondered why it had happened. I thought I'd done a pretty good job handling the sales department, competing with the bigger Vancouver radio market, exceeding sales budgets every month and getting the station recognized far beyond our broadcast borders. For three years we had even scooped up the World Hockey Association broadcast rights and sold them out. I thought things were going pretty well. I'd even made a costly personal investment in the station.

There is no question that the owner and I had philosophical differences and while I resented and strongly disagreed
with his reasons for my termination, it *was* his station and
he had every right to decide who would work for him and
who wouldn't. Clearly, I didn't fit into his plans and was
let go.

But you know what? Sometimes, actually quite often, a
cataclysmic thing like being fired can change your life. It
certainly changed mine.

My departure from that station was the catalyst for
actions that set me on a course of daring and courageous decisions — some of the biggest I had ever made.
Courageous? I was heavily in debt, my house was mort-
gaged to the hilt and I had cashed in all my life insurance to
buy 10 per cent of the station. And now I was on the street.
No golden handshake, no termination pay, nothing.

I'll admit, things were tough. For a while my parents
even dropped off hampers of food so my wife and I and
our very young daughter could eat. I was down about as
far as I could go. But I was not out!

I was watching *Gone With the Wind* one night when
something hit me. Halfway through the movie, Scarlett
was whipping her poor horse as it pulled her cart along the
road back to Tara. Hungry and exhausted, the horse died.

Scarlett got out of her buggy, fell to her knees, picked up
some earth and said, "As God is my witness, I will never
go hungry again."

In my own despair, I heard her message loud and clear.
The scene and Scarlett's words struck a chord in my heart

and I have repeated them to myself for more than 30 years.

I knew right then that I had to be fully responsible for the condition I now found myself in; it was I who had to be the architect of my own future. I could no longer blame the world, the station president, or any other "philosophical differences" real or imagined for what had happened. I had to get my life together, dream a better dream and take complete responsibility for all of my actions. I had to get up from the sorry state I was in and move forward.

I heard about a little magazine called *TV Week* that had gone into bankruptcy. Its printer, The Columbian Co., had inherited the publication when its printing bill went unpaid. While The Columbian had an interest in printing *TV Week*, the company was not interested in becoming its publisher. They needed a publisher.

When you're down, you need to be bold. I heard about the opportunity and coming from the media business and still considering myself to be a pretty good salesman, I approached the new owners to make a potential deal. I ended up buying 50 per cent of the magazine for the unpaid printing bill of $76,000. I would pay the bill out of subsequent profits.

My first day as publisher was April 3, 1976. In a rented back room of a Vancouver print shop, with a staff of just three, we went to work, assembling listings, selling advertising, developing editorial material and seeking a network to circulate the "we try harder" TV listings for a market that didn't really need us. When you have *TV Guide*, who needs *TV Week*?

At the time, no one expected that this humble foray into

Canadian publishing would put us on a fast track to success. We sold *TV Week* for 10 cents a copy and in the first year our sales topped $70,000. *TV Week* took on a giant, and with panache, style and enthusiasm, we began to beat him at his own game. We were local, we were different and we were better. Our initial success spurred new ventures. We began to gather the beginnings of a great army of enthusiasts who would nurture Canada Wide Media into maturity and make it the publishing force that it is today.

Our acquisitions and product development over the last 30-plus years have established our company as the largest independent magazine publisher in Western Canada. Our $30-million company now employs more than 130 media professionals in our Burnaby, B.C., headquarters and we have sales offices in Calgary and Toronto.

TV Week has become one of the highest paid-circulation entertainment and lifestyle magazines in Canada. From our beginning with one little title, we now publish 14 of our own magazines (including *BCBusiness*, *GardenWise* and *BC Home*) and 30 custom publications for leading clients serving business, consumer, leisure and trade markets. We have also diversified the company to include graphic design, web publishing, direct marketing, book publishing and fundraising.

Has everything we've done been entirely successful? No, it hasn't. But that's what being in business is all about — being able to revel in the successes and sweat through the difficulties, learning from our failures, mistakes and bad decisions to eventually make the company stronger and more successful in the future.

Looking back, I never would have imagined that losing the job that I had staked my future on — something that was completely devastating at the time — would lead me to the opportunity that would shape the rest of my life. I have to say, I am eternally thankful for that particular failure in my life.

4. Failure teaches us that we can survive a lot more than we imagine.
Failure is something to celebrate because it means that we have actually made an attempt at accomplishing something significant, we've stretched beyond our comfort zone and lived to tell about it. It builds our resilience and in realizing that we can survive a failure, we are more confident about pushing our own boundaries even further.

I remember my very first business failure, a tale some readers may recall from my earlier books. Like many entrepreneurs, I dreamed of being my own boss, calling the shots and ultimately building a hugely successful enterprise. But we all have to start somewhere and I started with a concession stand at the Pacific National Exhibition — the PNE, a large 17-day fair that takes place in Vancouver each summer. At the time, I had a full-time job at *The Columbian Newspaper* in New Westminster selling advertising but wanted to buy a second family car so my wife could have her own transportation while I was at work. Unfortunately, on my salary, a car for Kay seemed many years away.

Enter the business opportunity. Some associates of mine were selling a concession stand that they had run at the PNE the previous year. It was called Bunny's Foot Long

Hot Dogs and from the financials they provided, it looked like it had made a nice profit. It also appeared to be an easy 17-day venture that would allow me to get my feet wet running my own business and bring in the money necessary for a second car.

For a modest amount, I purchased the hot-dog stand and that's when my troubles began. Suddenly, I was bombarded with a host of problems I hadn't even begun to think about before handing over my money. For example, I had no idea who was going to manage the enterprise. I also didn't know where to order supplies or how much it would cost for stock. In addition, I would have to find staff to run the stand morning to night for the 17 days of the fair, not to mention negotiate a contract with the fair itself over their cut of the profits.

We eventually decided that my wife would be the one to run the stand, and I know you probably saw this coming, but at the time, with visions of easy money in my head, I didn't; that created the biggest problem of all: how was my wife going to get to work? She didn't have a car.

There was no way around it. We would have to buy a car before we had sold even one hot dog; so much for planning ahead. We settled on an Austin 1100, which cost around $475 and seemed like a great deal of money. The kicker was that we had to pay cash because we hadn't yet established a good credit rating.

In the end, my mom, dad and I all worked alongside Kay for 17 days straight from 10 a.m. to midnight. We also couldn't afford a babysitter, so Kay brought our young daughter Samantha with her every day to work.

I think Samantha must have eaten whatever profits there might have been that summer (we found out she really loves hot dogs). When the 17 days were over and the smell of grilled hot dogs had finally been washed out of our clothes, we barely broke even due to the fact that it rained every single day of the fair. Exhausted and happy that Kay at least had her car now, I happily returned to my job at the paper . . . at least until the next entrepreneurial idea hit.

Now, a lot of people might come away from that experience thinking, wow, I'm not very good at this whole business thing: the planning, the organization, the budgeting and the management, never mind dealing with all of the elements that are beyond my control like the weather and how many customers show up. Not me. I learned so many valuable lessons from that experience and I learned that failure isn't the end of the road. Perhaps the most important thing I learned from that summer selling hot dogs in the rain is that we should never be afraid to try a new venture because the only way we are going to develop the skills necessary to run a business is by actually doing it. Just like everything else in life, we learn by doing.

Of course, it is inevitable that we will make mistakes along the way, but hopefully we will also learn some valuable lessons and our mistakes will make us stronger, wiser and more confident that we can survive anything, even failure.

5. Failure teaches us to appreciate and savour our successes.
In the same way that sadness can teach us to appreciate the happy moments, failure provides us with something

to measure our successes against. As humans, we are designed to appreciate contrast. If we have too much of one thing, we want something else. If things are going along too smoothly, we'll do something to shake them up and make life more interesting. We like to have challenges, something to work towards and the sense of accomplishment that comes with conquering a difficult task. With each failure, we become more determined than ever to succeed and our eventual success is made all the more sweet for our struggle.

6. Failure teaches us perseverance.

Here is a quote from famous basketball player Michael Jordan: "I've missed more than 9,000 shots in my career. I've lost almost 300 games. Twenty-six times, I've been trusted to take the game-winning shot and missed. I've failed over and over and over again in my life. And that is why I succeed."

One of the greatest gifts of failure is the knowledge that failure is never final, unless we choose to give up.

At the age of eight, Nick Vujicic decided that he wanted to end his life. Born without arms or legs and unable to do many of the things that we all take for granted, he realized that he would not have a normal life — a job, a wife and family — and believed that he would also never be able to contribute to his community in a meaningful way. He decided to drown himself in the bathtub, but when it came down to the moment of truth, he couldn't do it. He thought about his parents and all of the love and support they had given him and also the guilt it would place on them if he killed himself.

Instead of giving up, which would have been quite understandable, Vujicic decided that there must be some other purpose for him and he set about discovering what that purpose could be. One day, after hearing the inspiring story of another man with severe disabilities, Vujicic realized that he had a great deal to share with the world — the story of his struggles, his triumphs (he enjoys boating, swimming, diving, fishing and golf), his incredible sense of humour and his inspirational message.

Today, he visits schools and talks to children of all ages about being thankful for what you do have, not bitter about what you don't have. It is especially touching to see the impact he has on teenaged audiences when he jokes around with them, demonstrates his many "abilities" and speaks to their biggest fears.

Discovering that we can turn our lives around, choose a different path or embrace a new idea at any age or in any set of circumstances is liberating and can motivate us to seek the wisdom and experience of others who have had different experiences, and can provide the momentum we need to propel us to successes beyond our imaginings.

Canadian artist and icon Emily Carr painted for years without critical success. In her early 40s, she decided to give up art and return to her hometown of Victoria in order to run a rooming house and breed dogs. For 15 years, she painted very little. Luckily for all who love her art, she met Lawren Harris of the Group of Seven, who encouraged her and renewed her interest in painting. As a result, Carr produced the work for which she is best known after the age of 57 and went on to have her art recognized for its "stunning originality and strength" and have it exhibited across Canada and in London, Paris, Washington and Amsterdam.

7. Failure teaches us to differentiate between what is important and what is not so important in our lives.
That's exactly what happened with author J.K. Rowling, leading her to finally sit down and write the Harry Potter series that subsequently turned her into a billionaire. In a moving speech she gave at Harvard on the topic of failure, Rowling described in her own words how hitting rock bottom, being unemployed and living on social assistance, finally helped her to fulfill her dream of being an author.

"So why do I talk about the benefits of failure?" she asked her audience. "Simply because failure meant a stripping away of the inessential. I stopped pretending to myself that I was anything other than what I was, and began to direct all my energy into finishing the only work that mattered to me. Had I really succeeded at anything else, I might never have found the determination to succeed in the one arena I believed I truly belonged. I was set free, because my greatest fear had already been realized, and I was still alive, and I still had a daughter whom I adored, and I had an old typewriter and a big idea. And so rock bottom became the solid foundation on which I rebuilt my life."

Failure has a way of focusing our attention like nothing else because we learn very quickly by experiencing it, what our priorities are. We learn what we can and can't live without, we discover our strengths, our weaknesses and our greatest desires. Essentially, our failures highlight our values and help us to define what is important in our lives. For example, the person who puts their family before all else and really works at building a successful home life, will probably not have a high-powered career, but will certainly have a close and nurturing relationship with their spouse and children. Likewise, the individual who thrives on building their career and putting in 80 or more hours a week will undoubtedly experience professional success, but surely their closest relationships will suffer as a result. Like the saying goes, it is possible to have everything we want in life, just not all at the same time. Therefore, we can use our failures to help us pinpoint and define what is most important so we can focus our time, energy and effort on that area and let the rest fall to the sidelines.

SOMETHING TO THINK ABOUT

Fear of making mistakes is one of the biggest obstacles to having an interesting and fulfilling life. The expectation that things need to go perfectly is unrealistic and extremely limiting. Not only are mistakes a wonderful source of insight that we can use to make progress towards fulfilling our dreams, at times they are absolutely necessary to make us stop and pay attention. Sometimes we have to hit that brick wall to realize that we need to try a different tack and discover other alternatives.

So next time you make a mistake, don't beat yourself up. Instead, be thankful for the insight you've been given and ask yourself, "How can I apply what I've learned?" No mistake should ever go to waste.

"Failure is, in a sense, the highway to success . . ."
— John Keats

"I have learned throughout my life as a composer chiefly through my mistakes and pursuits of false assumptions, not by my exposure to founts of wisdom and knowledge."
— Igor Stravinsky

Change your attitude towards failure

Why are you afraid of failure? Most people fear failure for one of two reasons. Either they believe that failure makes them a bad person, a "loser" that others look down on, or they are afraid that they will lose their money or possessions if they fail. Both of these are misconceptions.

Failure isn't a person; it's an event. When you fail, you are not a failure. A failure, even a significant one, doesn't magically wipe out all of your successes. Will others look down on you if you fail? Some people might, but you can't control the thoughts or actions of other people — so why worry about them?

As for losing all your money or possessions, there are more devastating things that could happen, like losing a loved one or your own health. Failure can be uncomfortable and unpleasant, but it is not life threatening. Nothing great is ever accomplished without the ever-present possibility of failure, and since we will never be able to outrun our fears, the best thing to do is face up to them. When we do, more often than not, we realize that they are not half as terrible as we imagined them to be.

So, put your doubts aside and go for it, because the only true failure is when you cease to try. Even when things don't work out as you expected, don't take it personally. Dust yourself off and move on. Learn from your mistakes and remember that failure always offers an opportunity of one kind or another — an opportunity to stretch beyond our usual boundaries, to learn something valuable or to make previously undreamed-of connections. Remembering this positive face of failure and focusing on it will go a long way towards changing your attitude about it. Once you accept that failure can actually be good for you, you're well on your way to a happier, more fulfilling life.

Turn a temporary defeat into victory

Alan Weiss has a new book entitled *Thrive! Stop Wishing Your Life Away.*

"Forget the people who were born on third base and think they have hit a triple," he says. "We all meet or see people daily who started with nothing or less (they were in debt) and rose to become successful.

"That's because they didn't allow their circumstances to become their excuse."

This includes failure, so turn this temporary defeat into victory.

CHAPTER 3

WHO ARE YOU TRYING TO PLEASE?

Let me ask you an important question. I want you to really think about it before you answer because it is absolutely critical to both your success and your happiness in life. Are you ready? Here's the question. Whose life are you living? Now, you might be inclined to answer right off the top of your head and say, "Well, mine of course." But are you really sure that it's not just the life your parents expected you to live, or the life your spouse wants, the life you think your children need you to live to provide for them, or perhaps even the life that your boss or a valued mentor thinks you should be living?

It's easy to get trapped by other people's expectations and easier still to be trapped by our own need for approval from those whom we love and respect. But living your life according to someone else's rules, making important decisions based on what others want rather than your own dreams and doing what is expected of you for the simple reason that you don't want to disappoint someone else is a recipe for unhappiness. You can't live someone else's life and sacrificing your own dream to please someone else simply leaves you exhausted and resentful. It takes courage to follow your own path in life and sometimes it can be a lonely journey.

Like many of us, Tsawwassen First Nation Chief Kim Baird sought out the advice of mentors as a young woman embarking on her career, but some of the advice she received didn't fit with her own values, and that created a problem.

"Earlier in my career, I actually had a mentor tell me I was naive because of my approach, because I wasn't pounding the table with my fist and that sort of thing," she says in an article about leadership in *BCBusiness Magazine*. "It really undermined my confidence for a period of time. I had to learn the hard way that I could be effective just being myself and since then I've been successful by following my own style of leadership. Ultimately, the best advice is something I've heard from many places, which is to be yourself. Now they have a fancy word for it: authenticity. It just means that you can be effective without having to have a persona. I've found that, as a young woman, I have a very collaborative style, which is not seen as typical of Indian chiefs and negotiators."

As a chief, one of Baird's biggest dreams has been to sign and implement British Columbia's first urban land treaty (Tsawwassen is located within the Metro Vancouver region) and she is now living that dream. As chief since 1999 (she has recently been re-elected for her sixth consecutive term in office), Baird represented her people throughout the negotiation process that ended in April 2009 with the signing of a treaty giving the Tsawwassen Nation full autonomy.

By staying true to herself and her own dream, Baird has accomplished something that many people believed impossible and she continues to pursue her dreams — based on her own values and doing it on her own terms.

Nobody but you can really tell you what you should do or what your dream should be. In fact, if you are someone with visionary ideas, chances are that most people won't even understand what it is that you want to accomplish. Take Henry Ford, inventor of the Model T automobile, as an example. "If I had asked people what they wanted, they would have said faster horses," said Ford, who had his own ideas about what the future of transportation would look like and used every opportunity he could to experiment and test his ideas. As a result of his vision and persistence, Ford designed a motor car that could be mass-produced using an improved assembly-line manufacturing process that he engineered himself and, as a result, brought motorized transportation to the masses.

Many people will tell you what you can't do, as illustrated by the following story from a book by John Maxwell: A salesman who was getting his hair cut casually mentioned to his barber that he was about to take a trip to Rome, Italy.

"Rome is a terribly overrated city," commented the barber, who was born in northern Italy. "What airline are you taking?"

The salesman told him the name of the airline and the barber responded, "What a terrible airline! Their seats are cramped, their food is bad and their planes are always late. What hotel are you staying at?"

The salesman named the hotel and the barber exclaimed, "Why would you stay there? That hotel is in the wrong part of town and has horrible service. You'd be better off staying home!"

"But I expect to close an important business deal while I am there," the salesman replied. "And afterwards I hope to see the pope."

"You'll be disappointed trying to do business in Italy," said the barber. "And don't count on seeing the pope. He only grants audiences to very important people."

Three weeks later the salesman returned to the barbershop.

"And how was your trip?" asked the barber.

"Wonderful!" replied the salesman. "The flight was perfect, the service at the hotel was excellent and I made a big sale. And . . ." The salesman paused for effect, "I got to meet the pope!"

"You got to meet the pope?" Finally, the barber was impressed. "Tell me what happened!"

"Well, when I approached him, I bent down and kissed his ring."

"No kidding! And what did he say?"

"He looked down at my head and said, 'My son, where did you ever get such a lousy haircut?' "

Hundreds of people will tell you what you can't do! Only a few will tell you what you can do. Who are you paying attention to?

If you study Hebrew, here's what it says about success: "It is the ability to make wise decisions."

That's it! Wise decisions.

It was my father's wise decision that brought me from England to British Columbia where I have found great success. You see, as a young man, he'd fought in the Second

World War and decided afterwards that his future lay somewhere other than England.

Having made that decision, he turned to my mother and asked, "Where should we go?"

"You've been around the world seven times," she said to him. "And the place you stopped the most was Vancouver. The ship you travelled on was also named *Vancouver City*, so let's move there."

As it turned out, that was a wise decision on the part of both of my parents.

In addition to his adventurous spirit, my father had a well-developed philosophy about success, which was based on seven basic principles. When I was 11 years old, he sat me down and shared them with me, and I have since shared them with countless others through my books and speeches:

1. Be resourceful, inventive and creative.
2. Carefully choose the five people that you spend the most time with.
3. Live every day with passion, a positive attitude and emotion. Never waste a day.
4. I won't always be with you, so seek out mentors who will teach you, encourage you and guide you.
5. Serve the community. Give back to the community infinitely more than you take out.
6. Set big goals.
7. Guard your integrity.

Finally, my father liked to quote Sir Winston Churchill when he so famously said, "It's not enough that we do our best, sometimes we have to do what's required."

Now, at the age of 11, it was hard for me to understand the value of all of this sage advice. However, as I watched my father's life unfold, it became clear to me that this was indeed very wise counsel. But there's a lot more to being successful than seven principles and a juicy quote. If we unpack these seven principles passed down from my father, I think we can find other successful people who can share similar wisdom.

1. Be resourceful, creative and inventive.

"The world needs men that have the courage to act on their own initiative. Moreover, men of this type write their own price tag and the world willingly pays it. The world willingly rewards men of initiative." — Andrew Carnegie

"Do what you do so well that when other people see what it is that you do, they will want to see you do it again and they will bring others with them to show them what it is that you do." — Walt Disney

2. Carefully choose the five people you spend the most time with.

Jean-Paul Sartre once said, "What is not possible is not to choose." The five people you spend the most time with influence you more than you might imagine. In fact, your income is the average of those five people. If you spend time with angry, negative, pessimistic people, guess what you're likely to become? So choose wisely when deciding to whom you will give your time and attention. Also remember that this rule applies to bosses and co-workers (whether you think so or not, you do have a choice about whom you work with and chances are during the course of a year you will spend more time with them than you do with most members of your own family).

3. Live every day with passion, a positive attitude and emotion — never waste a day.
The importance of a day can never be overstated, even the most ordinary days. I have been blessed in recent years with the addition of a new generation to my family. On most Tuesdays, I go into work a bit later than usual so that I can have breakfast at my home with my grandson Benjamin. Usually we have Eggo waffles. A few months ago, the two of us were sitting at the table enjoying our breakfast together and I was thinking about how much I look forward to this special time each week. I wanted to know if Benjamin felt the same way, so I asked him.

"Do you like having breakfast with Granddad?" I inquired.

"Yes, I really like it," he told me with a grin.

"Do you like the Eggos?" I asked.

"Yeah, Granddad," he replied, "I like the Eggos."

"What do you really love about it?" I asked (thinking, like most proud grandparents, that he would say something about spending time with me).

Without hesitation came his reply, "I really love the syrup, Granddad!"

These moments are a great reminder that we can't afford to waste a single day and we must be sure to celebrate the many milestones — both big and small — along the way, for we shall not pass this way again.

As for attitude, it really is everything in life. Research shows: 15 per cent of your success in life can be attributed to your technical skills. The other 85 per cent of your success is the result of your people skills and your ability to get along with others — to be real, to be you. Eighty-five per cent is a lot. I once heard, "Be who you is, 'cause if you ain't who you is, then you is who you ain't."

It costs to have a negative attitude. Attitude is a choice. If you've read *The Power to Soar Higher*, you've heard the story of Shed. I met Shed on a trip to St. Louis, Missouri, where I was giving a speech. He shines shoes for a living and as I was having my shoes shined, I asked him, "S-H-E-D, is that your real name or a nickname?"

"No," he said. "My name is Shed, my mama named me Shed . . . that's my name!"

I noticed he had a stethoscope around his neck. I said, "What's that for?"

"I is the doctor of shoes," he said. "I ain't lost a patient in 37 years. In fact, some people call me the saviour of soles."

And then I noticed a sign on his shoe-shine stand that said, "Shoe Shine: $2, Shoe Shine: $6."

"What's the difference?" I asked.

He said, "If you've got a good attitude, I charges you $2, but if you got a bad attitude, I charges you $6, cuz it costs to have a bad attitude."

4. Seek out mentors.
As my father said to me, find people with wisdom who are far more successful than you — who will teach you, guide

you, encourage you and hold you accountable. Take the very best of their habits and strategies and apply them to your own life and business.

I've been blessed with three mentors in my own life: Ray Addington, president of Kelly Douglas, who taught me the importance of following through; Mel Cooper, president and owner of CFAX Radio in Victoria, who taught me how to be creative and to say thank you; and Joe Segal, president of Kingswood Capital, who taught me the importance of how critical a person's 'word' is.

5. Serve the community.
Give back more than you take out. It's all part of the universal law of sowing and reaping.

Sow nothing, reap nothing.

If you plant temporary things, you will harvest temporary things.

If you plant generosity, you will harvest generosity.

If you offer grace and compassion, you will receive grace and compassion.

Whatever you give out in life is what you are going to get back.

Our legacy to the world can be whatever we choose it to be, it's up to us to decide. But keep in mind our actions will speak louder than any words. There is a famous quote from Nelson Henderson that sums it up nicely, "The true meaning of life is to plant trees under whose shade you do not expect to sit."

6. Have big goals.

If you're going to dream, dream big. Don't just think outside the box — as my friend Nido Qubein, president of
High Point University in North Carolina, once said —
throw the box away. Fewer than one-half of one per cent
of business leaders have specific goals.

You can walk up and down the main street of any city
and ask almost anyone, "Do you have any goals?" Most
will say no, others will say, "Yes, I want to be rich and
happy." If they say that, ask them if they have any idea
how to get there. Most likely, they will say no.

Goals must be balanced. If it's all about the money,
eventually you will end up feeling unhappy and dissatisfied.
Goals need to include career aspirations, hopes and dreams
for your family, your health, spiritual and educational
goals.

Dr. Benjamin E. Mays, the late president of Morehouse
College near Atlanta, once said:

"It must be borne in mind that the tragedy in life doesn't
lie in not reaching your goals, the tragedy lies in having
no goals to reach. It isn't a calamity to die with dreams
unfulfilled, but it is a calamity not to dream. It is not a
disaster to be unable to capture your ideal, but it is a disaster to have no ideal to capture. It is not a disgrace not to
reach the stars, but it is a disgrace to have no stars to reach
for."

7. Guard your integrity.

Above all, the most important principle of success is integrity. I've left this to last because it is the most important. In

everything you do, demand complete integrity and ethical behaviour. American author John Maxwell said, "There is no such thing as business ethics . . . it is all ethics."

When you have integrity and all of the values that go with it such as honesty, loyalty, team appreciation, fairness, courage and compassion, you will find that people trust you and will want to do business with you.

Do not compromise on integrity! It takes 25 years to build a reputation but just five minutes to destroy it. Guard your reputation. In reality, it's the most important thing you will ever have.

"A reputation once broken may possibly be repaired, but the world will always keep their eyes on the spot where the crack was."

— Joseph Hall

SOMETHING TO THINK ABOUT

It's easy to make excuses for why we aren't pursuing our own dreams. "I'm too busy working and earning a living to think about what I really want; I don't have time to set goals; I'd need to go back to school; it's too complicated; my spouse would never understand; it's too late to start over in a new career; I wouldn't be good enough to make a living doing what I enjoy; there's too much competition."

All of these comments come from a place of fear. Some people are afraid of accomplishment or they worry that if they fulfill their potential, they will alienate others. Some people are afraid of the responsibility of living up to their destiny. They know they have the potential to do great things, but they're afraid of what that means. "Consult not your fears, but your hopes and your dreams," said Pope John XXIII. "Think not about your frustrations, but about your unfulfilled potential. Concern yourself not with what you tried and failed in, but with what it is still possible for you to do."

I have a challenge for you. I want you to sit down right now and answer the question I asked at the beginning of this chapter.

"Whose life are you living?"

Give it some serious thought and if you're not happy with the answer, it's time to do something about that.

"This is your life, are you who you want to be?"
— Switchfoot (from the lyrics to "This is Your Life")

CHAPTER 4

WHAT BURNS IN YOUR SOUL?

Doug Morneau is the Chief Rhino for Rhino Marketing Inc. His kids are at the age where they are just deciding what career path they want to pursue. Over lunch recently, he shared with me the advice he gave to them about choosing a career.

"Find something that will wake you up a half-hour before the alarm," he told them.

Essentially, what he is telling them is not to settle for a job or career, but to discover what it is that they are truly passionate about and go for it.

Excellent advice; research shows that for entrepreneurs, the No. 1 indicator of success is not knowledge or experience — it is passion. The same holds true for most endeavours in life. What gets an athlete out of bed at five in the morning to run 10 miles in the dark? What inspires a pilot to log 2,000 hours of flight time to get a commercial license? What motivates a teacher to stand in front of a class of noisy, boisterous children day after day with a smile?

I can tell you, it isn't just the money; it isn't just the respect of one's colleagues and competitors; it isn't just the knowledge that our services are needed. It takes more than that. What it is, is a driving force that burns deep inside, pushing us forward through all of the difficulties and all of the challenges. It is a desire to be the best and to break new ground. It is knowing that we are on the path we were meant to take. It is the incredible feeling that this is what we were made to do. I get that feeling every time I step up onto a stage to speak to an audience, I know that it is what I was born to do and that's the reason I am still doing it with enthusiasm 40 years later.

I'm not the only one, of course. Even after 25 years, it is impossible not to be impressed with Rick Hansen, a man who is perhaps best known as "The Man in Motion." With his determined, inspirational, heart-stopping, 34-country, four-continent, 40,000 km wheelchair journey in 1985, he made history and raised $26 million to support research to help people living with spinal cord injuries.

As the guest of Langley mayor Rick Green's *Complete Champion* lunch program in the brand new Langley Events Centre, along with 300 others, I listened once again to Rick Hansen's amazing story.

Over the years, he has lost none of his humility or his passion for his life's mission — today he is CEO of the Rick Hansen Foundation. To date he has helped raise more than $200 million to improve quality of life and fund projects, awareness programs and resources.

Here are some excerpts from his presentation:

"Focus on things you can do, not the things you can't do. The key is focus."

"It's not a physical limitation, it's a mental limitation."

The highlight for me was when Hansen talked about the moments during his journey where he felt as if he could go no further.

"Those bitter winter days on the prairies battling minus-50-degree temperatures — asking myself, is this really all worth it? I can't go on, I'm going to quit — asking myself, do I have one more stroke in me and then another and another and seeing the incredible potential each of us has if we don't quit."

Then he turned to the audience to say: "Do you have one more stroke in you?"

"I honestly believe my best work is in the front, not behind me," he told us. "I'm driven by wanting to make a difference and leave this world a little better than when I arrived." Fuelled by his mantra, "anything is possible."

The powerful and emotional close to his presentation was David Foster's "The Power of the Dream" composition sung by Céline Dion while pictures of Hansen's inspiring journey played across the screen. As his life journey evolves, he just sets the bar even higher, asking himself and asking all of us, "What are you going to do while you're here, with your every breath?"

March 21, 2010, marked the 25th anniversary of the day that Hansen and his team departed Vancouver's Oakridge Centre on the Man in Motion World Tour. To celebrate he announced the creation of the Rick Hansen Institute, which will connect people and countries around the world in order to make significant contributions towards spinal cord injury research and care. He also announced the launch of a 25th-anniversary campaign to raise a further $200 million for the institute and other programs that support spinal cord research, another big goal and a commitment to continue to make the most of every moment and every breath.

How do you feel about what you do every day? What are you going to do while you're here, with your every breath? Take a few minutes to really think about that. How do you truly feel? Are you excited to get up each morning? Do your plans for the day wake you up half an hour before the alarm and make you want to jump out of bed and get going because there's not a moment to waste? Do you know for a fact that there's nothing else you would rather be doing with your life? Are you using every breath wisely?

I hope so, because the success of any dream hinges on the amount of passion we have to make it happen. If you don't feel the kind of passion that gets your heart racing with excitement when you think of all you want to accomplish, it's time to ask some questions and make some changes.

A Korn/Ferry International survey of global executives found that half wished they could start over in a different career. That statistic in itself is not surprising, it can take a lot of exploring to figure out what we want. The unfortunate reality is that many of those who are unhappy or unfulfilled in their career will never do anything about it. They'll never know what dreams might have been waiting to be discovered.

In *The Tempest*, Shakespeare wrote, "We are such stuff as dreams are made on."

The Vancouver 2010 Olympic Games were such stuff and what started as one man's dream soon became the dream of thousands.

Thirteen years ago, Bruce MacMillan of Tourism Vancouver walked down the hall to Tourism Vancouver president Rick Antonson's office. Leaning on the door-jamb, he said to Rick, "I have an idea, I have a dream."

"What is it?" Rick asked.

"Why don't we put together a bid for the right to hold the 2010 Winter Olympics?" Bruce replied.

"Yes," said Rick.

The power of yes is needed to move any dream forward; nobody ever remembers who says no. Because of this dream, which was fuelled by action, earlier this year, Canada hosted a spectacular and memorable Winter Olympic and Paralympic Games.

To make it happen, Rick Antonson, who worked on the production of *TV Week* in its formative years, teamed up with local movers and shakers David Bentall, Brian Dolsen, former B.C. premier Glen Clark, Joy MacPhail and former Vancouver mayor Philip Owen. This was the original dream team who envisioned the Winter Olympics for Vancouver.

Looking for a high-profile business leader, they convinced Arthur Griffiths, who at the time owned the Vancouver Canucks, to be that person.

With $100,000 from Tourism Vancouver, another $100,000 from the Province of British Columbia and Griffiths using his personal credit card to pay for ongoing expenses — not even knowing if the expenses would be repaid — they set about accomplishing this Big Dream.

Vancouver first beat out Quebec City and Calgary for the Canadian National bid, then worked earnestly to convince the International Olympic Committee to award the 2010 Winter Olympic Games to Vancouver.

The rest, as they say, is history.

On Friday, February 12, 2010, at 6 p.m. Pacific Standard Time, the 2010 Olympic Opening Ceremonies began in front of 60,000 Olympic fans and about three billion viewers worldwide.

A monumental dream was realized!

During a pre-Olympic event at Vancouver's Queen Elizabeth Theatre, Canada's Governor General, Michaelle Jean, O.C., declared, "The very best we have to give, will be given."

And it was, thanks to the organizers, athletes, volunteers, sponsors, supporters and millions of Canadians who got in the spirit and welcomed the world with open arms.

The Olympics were one of the most inspiring and exciting things that have ever happened in Vancouver.

I'm reminded that a dozen or so years ago, my wife and I were travelling on the cruise ship, *Island Princess*. We visited Istanbul, Athens, Crete, the Holy Land, Egypt and Rome. During our short one-day visit to Athens, our tour guide took us downtown to the site of the Olympic stadium where we all had the opportunity to run a lap around the entire track. It was both exciting and exhilarating to find ourselves in the birthplace of the very first Olympic Games.

Little did I realize at the time that seven years later (on July 2, 2003, while I was chair of the 4,500-member Vancouver Board of Trade), Vancouver's bid to host the 2010 Olympic and Paralympic Winter Games would catapult our city — and our country — onto the world stage.

On that day, we were hosting VIPs, sponsors and

dignitaries at the World Trade Centre suite in GM Place stadium when International Olympic Committee president Jacques Rogge made the famous announcement, live from Prague, that the 2010 Winter Games had been awarded to the city of Vancouver.

The crowd of 20,000-plus anxious early risers at GM Place went absolutely wild with excitement. In the suite, we shared tears of joy, coupled with plenty of handshakes and hugs as we toasted our city's victory with champagne and orange juice.

Nearly seven years later, the Vancouver Organizing Committee (VANOC), our athletes, sponsors, Canadian fans and everyone else associated with the 2010 Olympics did us proud by putting on the best Games possible. It was our time to welcome the world and a quarter-million visitors and billions of television viewers across the globe got a taste of all that B.C. has to offer — friendly people, a thriving economy, natural beauty and wonderful communities.

VANOC CEO John Furlong, who immigrated to Canada many years ago from his home in Ireland, has often shared the story of his arrival here. Upon his entry into Canada, the immigration officer who examined his passport looked him in the eye and said, "Welcome to Canada. Make us better." As leader of the team orchestrating the massive undertaking that was the 2010 Games, John has indeed done his part to make our country better.

Following the Olympics, John had this to say about his experience.

"I have an even greater appreciation today than I've ever had in my life about the power of a vision and about what happens when people pursue something with the kind of vigour you can. I think something pretty extraordinary has happened in the country and I am glad to have been a part of it."

I believe many, many Canadians share his sentiment. Dreams are powerful things — they can inspire us to accomplish amazing feats. As the Olympic torch run began, Canadians across the country witnessed the culmination of a shared dream based on years of planning, preparation and hard work. In whatever small way they could, they wanted to be a part of that dream, whether they were running with the Olympic torch (in total, nearly 12,000 people participated in the longest relay in the history of the Olympics), volunteering at the Games (people travelled from all across the country and from other countries to give their time) or simply cheering on the athletes, each of whom had a dream of their own.

At last year's *BCBusiness Magazine* TOP 100 event at the Hotel Vancouver celebrating the year's leading local companies, the keynote speaker was former women's Olympic ice-hockey captain Cassie Campbell. During her presentation, she described the incredible discipline and other attributes that it takes to win a gold medal — the constant training, practice, persistence, dedication and intensity. She said that every country in the world knew that if they had any expectations of getting into the gold-medal hockey round, they had to go through Canada first. Her team had set a standard and others knew that if they hoped to measure up, they too would have to meet and exceed that standard.

That's what dreams do for us; they set a standard we can aspire to. They burn in our soul, making us yearn with every ounce of our being, forcing us to go beyond our comfort zone, pushing our limits and testing our strength . . . to see what we are truly made of. If you haven't yet discovered what burns in your soul, ask yourself these four questions:

1. What would I do if I had no limitations?
2. What would I do if I only had five years to live?
3. What would I do if I had unlimited resources?
4. What would I do if I knew I couldn't fail?

Despite what we believe we should focus on in our waking hours, sometimes our dreams have other plans for us and it is in our best interest to let the dream lead the way. After graduating from UBC, my friend Lorne Segal proceeded to study law at Oxford University in England where, based upon the Socratic method, his studies required him to read a thousand pages twice a week and then write an essay discussing what he had learned from his readings. It was a daunting task and more often than not, he found himself walking the streets of the distinguished university at two or three in the morning searching for inspiration. It was during these walks that he began to marvel at the great architecture of the place and ask himself, "Why doesn't anyone build like this anymore?" He also began to realize during those early morning walks that his heart was not in the study of law. What he really yearned to do was create a unique building that took the best architectural elements of the past and combined them with the technology of the present.

So, each night as he slept, his vision of the "Kingswood" (as it would be called 27 years later) began to grow and take shape in his mind. Although he didn't know anything about real estate or property development, he knew that he had to follow his passion and someday, somehow, realize his dream. Returning home to Vancouver, Lorne acquired his real estate license and started to learn the business, eventually moving from the residential to the commercial sector. Later, he founded Kingswood Properties and having accumulated enough knowledge and experience to realize his vision, began plans for building his dream.

It was a five-year journey that involved an in-house team of 28 students and architects focused on nothing but the project. During that time, Lorne slept with a roll of tracing paper next to his bed so that he could quickly sketch ideas or make changes that came to him as he slept. The next morning, those changes would be incorporated into the plan and the process would continue. In all, close to 10,000 pages were marked up in this way before the project was complete. Designers and artisans, stonemasons, millworkers, glass cutters and painters set up workshops on the grounds. It was a magnificent obsession that culminated in a spectacular 12-storey building that is home to 18 handcrafted homes that could rival any of Europe's most elegant residences.

All who have seen it would agree, the Kingswood truly is a masterpiece and a beautiful jewel in Vancouver's crown. If you haven't seen the building, it is located at 1596 West 14th Avenue adjacent to the Vancouver Lawn Tennis and Badminton Club. For Lorne, the dream came full circle when he was invited to Buckingham Palace earlier this year after corresponding with the Prince of Wales regarding his inspiration for the Kingswood.

You really are the master of your destiny

Whenever someone shares a shoulda, coulda, woulda story with me — you know, a story about all the things that have kept them from doing what they really want to do in life (such as doubting family and friends, wrong circumstances, lack of opportunity, etc.), I am reminded of the following story.

One day, a traveller from a far and distant town approached a wise man who was just leaving the city into which the traveller was entering. The traveller stopped the wise man and said, "Can you tell me about the city from whence you have just come? What is the quality and character of the citizens here?"

The wise man replied, "First, stranger, tell me: What were the people like in the last town you visited?"

The traveller was quick to reply, "Oh, they were a cold bunch of people with no kind words for anyone. It was not a happy town; they were very judgmental and the people were mean spirited and unwelcoming. I couldn't get out of that town fast enough."

The wise man paused and then responded, "Ahhh . . . I

believe you will discover that the citizens of this town are exactly the same."

A short distance further down the road, the wise man encountered another traveller heading towards the city. And likewise, the traveller asked the same question of the wise man, saying, "What is the quality and character of the citizens of this city, sir?"

Again, the wise man replied, "First, stranger, tell me: What were the people like in the last town you visited?"

Without hesitation, the traveller responded, "Oh, they were an amazing group of people! They were outgoing and friendly and welcomed me with open arms. They were unconditionally loving and I felt like each one was my brother or sister . . . . Oh, I miss them greatly."

The wise man paused and then replied, "Ahhh . . . I believe you will discover that the citizens of this town are exactly the same."

Too often, we put the responsibility for our aspirations and expectations on others when we have far more control over what we experience than we give ourselves credit for. We are the masters of our own destiny. The life we experience is the one we've chosen; otherwise we would be somewhere else doing something else. What we need to remember is that we tend to get back what we put out. If we put out negativity, that's what we're likely to get back. If we choose to see obstacles rather than challenges, then life will likely be much more difficult than it needs to be. When we look for the good in people and situations, we can always find it just as when we look for the bad, we can find that too. It's up to each one of us to decide what kind of experience and what kind of life we are going to choose.

—⁄⁄⁄—

More than 15 years ago, I made a very smart decision. I bought *BCBusiness* from Jimmy Pattison, a magazine that has become a cornerstone of my publishing business, Canada Wide Media Limited, and also the most successful regional business magazine in Canada. A number of months ago we did a feature looking at nearly 20 of British Columbia's most successful individuals (from many walks of life) and the advice that most helped each of them get to where they are today. I've always believed that we can learn a great deal from those who have travelled the path ahead of us and so I have chosen several of these stories to share with you within the pages of this book.

The first of these stories is about a man I admire greatly, the Vancouver Symphony Orchestra's musical director, Bramwell Tovey. Born in England like myself, Tovey's success isn't dependent upon a magic wand (though it might sometimes seem that way when he is up on the stage conducting the orchestra), nor was he born with a silver spoon in his mouth. Yet he is most definitely living the dream that he imagined for himself as a young man just starting out on his career path in the U.K.

How did he do it? The answer comes in two parts.

First of all, he acted on some good advice from someone

who had been down the path before him (the creator of the Los Angeles Opera, Peter Hemmings). The advice he received was to get out of the public eye and go work somewhere remote where he could focus on learning the repertoire of a conductor, top to bottom, front to back. Tovey did just that in 1989 when he accepted a position as artistic director of the Winnipeg Symphony. The second reason for his success is good, old-fashioned hard work. As Tovey himself says, it doesn't matter how good a musician you are, as a conductor you still have to learn the ropes.

The same holds true for every dream. Wanting to be a chef or a doctor or even a public speaker doesn't make you one; you need to have a fire inside you that drives you to do everything you can to make your dream come true.

As I mentioned in Chapter 1, I am often approached by people who say to me, "Peter, I want to be a successful public speaker, travelling around the world and speaking to large audiences just like you do. How can I make it happen?"

My response never changes. There is no magic formula, whatever it is that you want to do, you have to want it enough that you are willing to start at the bottom, taking every opportunity you can to build your skills to the point where people are willing to pay you money to do what you love. You also have to love it enough that you want to keep learning and keep getting better. Even after so many years, I still consider myself to be a journeyman speaker, always learning, always wanting to get better at my craft, always seeking out masters of the craft to learn from. It's a lifelong journey and passion is the fuel that keeps me moving forward.

My good friend and mentor Joe Segal, president of Kingswood Capital Corporation, has always dreamed big and during a career that has spanned nearly seven decades, he's made his dreams come true (if you'd like to know more about Joe's story, pick up my book *The Runway of Life*, which was inspired by Joe's personal philosophy of life). In addition to his willingness to share his time and wisdom with me, the thing that I have always most admired about Joe is that he's a man who has definitely got his priorities straight, as evidenced by a long and happy marriage, a wonderful family and a life well lived. Joe shared the following story with me one day over lunch, which I included in an early volume of *If Only I'd Said That*. I think the story really speaks to Joe's philosophy:

A professor stood before his philosophy class with a number of items in front of him. When the class began, wordlessly, he picked up a very large and empty mayonnaise jar and proceeded to fill it with golf balls.

He then asked the students if the jar was full. They agreed that it was.

The professor then picked up a box of pebbles and poured them into the jar. He shook the jar lightly. The pebbles rolled into the open areas between the golf balls. He asked the students again if the jar was full. They agreed it was.

Next, the professor picked up a box of sand and poured it into the jar.

Of course, the sand filled up everything else. He asked

once more if the jar was full. The students responded with a unanimous yes.

The professor then produced two glasses of red wine from under the table and poured the entire contents into the jar, effectively filling the empty spaces between the grains of sand. The students laughed.

"Now," said the professor as the laughter subsided, "I want you to recognize that this jar represents your life. The golf balls are the important things: your family, your children, your health, your friends and your favourite passions; things that if everything else were lost and only they remained, your life would still be full.

"The pebbles are the other things that matter, like your job, your house and your car. The sand is everything else: the small stuff.

"If you put the sand into the jar first," he continued, "There is no room for the pebbles or the golf balls. The same goes for life. If you spend all your time and energy on the small stuff, you will never have room for the things that are important to you.

"Pay attention to the things that are critical to your happiness. Play with your children. Take time to get medical checkups. Take your partner out to dinner. Play another 18 holes of golf. Do one more run down the ski slope. There will always be time to clean the house and fix the faucet. Take care of the golf balls first, the things that really matter. Set your priorities. The rest is just sand."

One of the students then raised her hand and inquired what the wine represented.

The professor smiled. "I'm glad you asked. It just goes

to show you that no matter how full your life may seem, there's always room for a couple of glasses of wine with a friend."

Each of us needs to figure out what is most important to us, to discover what our passion or passions are and then make sure that we make space in our life for those before we fill up that space with other, less significant things.

—m—

I truly enjoy meeting and learning from people who have found their own way to pursue a particular passion. I was in Cardiff, Wales, earlier this year, taking a small sojourn during a business trip to London to visit with family. I booked my return trip from Cardiff to London on the train and the morning of my departure, I was enjoying a full English breakfast at the Cardiff Marriott, which is just down the block from the train station. Although I know it's not good for me, I love my full English breakfast, which, for those who don't know, consists of sausage, eggs, English bacon, baked beans, fried bread and mushrooms. As I sat eating, I noticed that the walls were covered with photographs of famous Welsh folks including singers Tom Jones and Shirley Bassey, football players Ben Burns and Ryan Gates, Cardiff City football coach John Toshack and Olympic runner Colin Jackson. In between the pictures were quotations, nicely framed. One that caught my eye was from Charles Dickens, "A day wasted on others is not wasted on self."

I copied it down in my notebook, sure that I would use it somewhere in the future, although I had no idea when or where. Having finished my meal, I gathered my bags and walked over to the station. Arriving at Cardiff Central Station with my first-class ticket for the noon train in hand, I was ushered into the first-class lounge, which is part of the 1934 rebuilt station. Now, don't be misled, it may have been called a first-class lounge, but in reality it was a small, unimposing room whose most important function was to provide passengers with shelter from the inclement Welsh wind and rain.

As I walked in, the congenial hostess, Lena McSorley, asked if I would like coffee, orange juice or a muffin before looking at my ticket and confirming the departure platform and time of my train.

"Just relax," she told me. "The train will be here in 45 minutes."

Noticing that I was the only passenger in the lounge at the time, I settled into a comfortable chair and surveyed my surroundings. On the wall beside me was a certificate stating, "Lena McSorley has been voted Cardiff's Best Ambassador for 2009." Looking over at Lena, I saw nothing more than a regular, straightforward, simply spoken person, but eventually my curiosity got the better of me, so I asked her how this came about.

With a sense of humility, she produced a certificate from the Prince's Trust congratulating her on having raised £1,221.19 in 2005. She then produced a certificate from the Velinare Cancer Treatment Hospital for which she raised £5,800 in 2006. In 2007, she raised £500 for the Alzheimer's Society of Wales. In 2008, she raised £3,868.14 for children suffering from cancer and leukemia. In 2009, she raised £2,000 for sexually abused children in Cardiff and in the same year, a further £4,068.75 for the Children's Therapy Clinic in Wales. That's almost $30,000 Canadian.

My next questions for Lena were how and why? Her response: "I've been married for 16 years, my husband is retired and I feel very lucky with life. I've had no health problems or family problems and I feel it's a privilege to be running this first-class lounge at Cardiff Central Station."

As Martin Luther King Jr. once said:

"Everybody can be great, because anybody can serve. You don't have to have a college degree to serve. You don't have to make your subject and your verb agree to serve. You don't have to know about Plato and Aristotle to serve. You don't have to know Einstein's theory of relativity to serve. You don't have to know the second law of thermo-dynamics in physics to serve. You only need to have a heart full of grace. A soul generated by love."

Clearly, Lena McSorley has a soul generated by love and she simply asks those who come into the lounge if they can help her current project. No expenses, no elaborate bro-chures and no overhead, just a friendly, genuine woman who cares for her community. Maybe she too has read the Charles Dickens quote on the wall of the Cardiff Marriott breakfast room and taken it to heart, because she's cer-tainly not one to waste a day on herself and, in so doing, Lena discovered her own passion for helping others.

What burns in your soul?

The truth is, you're the only one who can even hope to answer that question. If you're not happy with the life you have, you owe it to yourself to make it better, to pursue whatever it is that provides you with a sense of fulfillment and purpose. Even if it means setting aside the expectations that you believe others have for you — whether those expectations come from your parents, your spouse, your friends or even your children — there are no acceptable excuses. The reality is that each of us only has a finite amount of time in this life, so there isn't any to waste. It is time to give yourself permission — to dream, to aspire, to hope for the best and to make your dream a reality.

SOMETHING TO THINK ABOUT

We all have many dreams we would like to come true and there's no reason that we can't make them happen. As you prepare to pursue your dreams, keep in mind that a clear dream makes a general idea very specific. Consider the following statements:

- I want to lose weight.
- I want to have a better relationship with my children.
- I really should finish my university degree so I can get a better job.
- I want to get out of debt.
- I ought to get in shape.
- I need to improve my leadership skills.
- I should learn a second language.
- I want to start my own business.

These are all general ideas/dreams but they aren't going

to get you very far. To start things moving in the right direction, you need a clear picture of what you want to achieve and an action plan to get started. Give yourself a specific goal and a time frame to work within.

Here are some examples based on the previous list:

- I will adjust my daily calorie intake to reduce my weight by one pound per week for the next six months and search the Internet for information on healthy eating.
- I will schedule one evening every week and one day of every weekend to enjoy activities with my children.
- I will take one course each semester until I complete my degree and join a networking group to help improve my job prospects.
- I will pay off 10 per cent of my credit card debt each month and not take on any new debt until it is completely repaid.
- I will swim for 30 minutes every weekday and invite friends to join me for at least one walk, hike or sports activity on weekends.
- I will read one leadership book every month and seek out a mentor to learn from.
- I will study Chinese for an hour each day and enrol in a conversational Chinese class.
- During the next three months, I will research and write a business plan for my new business.

What can you do right now to make your dream clearer?

"If you don't know where you're going, any road will get you there."

— The Cheshire Cat (*Alice in Wonderland*)

CHAPTER 5

WHAT ARE YOU WILLING TO SACRIFICE FOR YOUR DREAM?

Many people say they have a dream, but are not ready to do what is required to get there. In life there is always a price for what we want to accomplish. My experience tells me it takes twice as much money and three times longer, or three times as much money and two times longer, than we expect for a dream to get off the ground. Once you have determined what your dream is, stand firm on your commitment. It takes more than wishing to realize your dream.

Those of you who have read *The Runway of Life* may recall my son-in-law Trevor and his dream to become a medical doctor.

Trevor married my youngest daughter Amanda in July 2000. Amanda is one of those people others often envy for the fact that she knew from a young age that she wanted to be a teacher and she has been living her dream ever since she graduated from university. Although he was very successful in his career working for a technology company, Trevor did not feel the same way about his chosen career, and seven years ago, things came to a head.

Trevor and Amanda came to see us on a Sunday and Amanda was in tears as the two of them explained their dilemma. With a beautiful home and plans to start a family in the near future, they would literally have to turn their lives upside down to accommodate Trevor's dream.

As we sat discussing their options, I laid out the facts as I saw them.

"If this is truly your dream, you're going to have to sell your home and downsize to an 800-square-foot apartment. You'll also have to sell one of your cars and get used to taking transit. Next, Trevor will have to enrol at Simon Fraser University and get straight A's in order to get into a good medical school. Meanwhile, Amanda is going to have to be the breadwinner, at least for a couple of years. Once he's completed all of the science requirements, the next step for Trevor will be getting into a medical school, hopefully UBC. Once he gets accepted at a university, that's when the real work begins — four years of medical school, followed by the decision of whether or not to specialize and then another four years as an intern. It's going to require a lot of sacrifices from both of you and it's a long road ahead."

With a clear plan of action and the emotional support of both their families, Trevor and Amanda embarked on a new journey together. Seven years later, Trevor has completed medical school at UBC and decided to pursue a career as an ear, nose and throat specialist. He was also very fortunate to secure an internship at Vancouver General Hospital where he is currently one-and-a-half years into his four-year-term.

In the meantime, he and Amanda have had two children — a son, Benjamin, and a daughter, Cate — and they couldn't be happier with the life they are making together.

It hasn't always been easy and everything hasn't always gone as planned, but Trevor and Amanda both believed in Trevor's dream enough that they were willing not only to make sacrifices in their lifestyle but also to take on the student loans necessary to make that dream come true.

As Trevor's story clearly illustrates, it takes more than wishing to realize a dream and it takes more than saying you want something to make it happen.

I'm sure you've done your fair share of wishing and wanting . . .

- I wish I had more money.
- I want a more fulfilling job.
- I wish I had a university education.
- I wish I would get a promotion.
- I want a better relationship with my spouse.
- I wish that I were happier.
- I want to be healthy.
- I wish I could retire early.
- I want to travel around the world.
- I wish I had gone to university and earned a degree.

Many people stick it out in a job they dislike for years, decades, sometimes even their entire career, all the while wishing and wondering about the thing they really wanted to do, the leap of faith they were too afraid to take. Dreams don't happen without risk and time spent waiting for the perfect circumstances to turn up is time wasted. It's time to move beyond wishing and wanting. If your dream is important, you're going to have to decide what your priorities are and make some sacrifices to get the life you want, whether it means going back to school to get your degree, giving up an unsatisfactory job to do something you love for less money or moving to a new city to find the opportunity you want. Your dream isn't going to happen until and unless you're willing to do what it takes.

Something terrible happens when you don't take action . . . NOTHING!

It's time to make some important choices. If you're really serious about your dream, here are five questions worth asking:

- What am I willing to pay for my dream?
- How soon am I willing to pay it?
- How will I handle criticism and naysayers?
- How will I overcome my own fears to make it happen?
- How hard am I willing to work to make my dream come true?

These are tough questions and it may take time to find the answers, but once you do, you will realize that the pieces needed to build your dream are beginning to fall into place.

Broadcaster Paul Harvey often said: "You can always tell when you are on the road to success: It's uphill all the way. If you have no problems, it's a path that leads nowhere."

On the last four or five books that I've published, I've had the pleasure of working with Tashon Ziara. I first met Tashon during my tenure as chair of the Vancouver Board of Trade. As a freelance writer who's been working with the Board for more than a decade, each year Tashon collaborates with the chair to write their recurring column in the Board's member publication *Sounding Board*, in addition to providing support for speeches and other presentations.

Tashon and I got along famously during my year as chair and I appreciated her ability to take my stories and weave them into a speech or an article. When it came time to start work on my next book, I didn't hesitate to ask Tashon if she would like to work with me.

Over time, I learned the story of how she made her own dream of being a professional writer come true.

With a one-year-old son in tow and pregnant with her second child, Tashon and her husband moved from Vancouver to Calgary in 1997. With no contacts in the city and needing to work for financial reasons, she took the only job she could find, working in a funeral home.

In addition to an array of duties that included arranging for the pick-up and transfer of deceased persons to the funeral home, updating the funeral directors' schedule and handling the administration of incoming and outgoing cremated remains, one of Tashon's regular tasks was to interview the families of deceased persons and write obituaries that could be sent to the local newspapers.

Despite having what many people would consider a macabre work environment, Tashon told me she found she truly enjoyed talking with the families and hearing their stories. More to the point, she enjoyed writing the obituaries in which the whole of a person's life had to be captured in a few short paragraphs and she discovered that she had a real talent for it. In her words, it was like writing a series of mini biographies.

Just two months before her second son was born, Tashon and her husband separated and she returned to Vancouver having no idea how she was going to support two children once her maternity benefits ran out. With only two years of college and no degree or special skills, it was going to be tough to find a job that would cover full-time childcare for two little ones and pay the bills.

Realizing that she would rather have a hand up than a handout, a few months after her second son was born, Tashon applied to participate in a federal government program that offered sponsorship to anyone with an expired employment insurance claim for education or training to help them find long-term stable employment. Having come across an article about a two-year writing program offered by Douglas College, she made up her mind that she was going to follow a dream that she had had since grade school: she was going to become a professional writer.

Even with the knowledge that this was an investment in her future and the future of her children, the next two years of Tashon's life weren't going to be easy. She was grateful to receive the funding needed to go back to school despite the fact that doing so meant there would be many sleepless nights ahead and she would have to make the most of every dollar in her monthly budget — more than half of which would be needed to pay for a caregiver for the boys while she was at school.

The writing program turned out to be much more demanding than Tashon could have imagined. With a full course load, she adjusted her schedule, going to sleep at 7 p.m. with the boys so that she could get up at 11 p.m. to study through the night in preparation for the next day's classes. While her classmates enjoyed leisurely lunches and evening get-togethers, Tashon rushed home each day to spend time with her children, in addition to cooking, cleaning and taking care of all the other household chores. Thankfully, she found an outlet in her writing assignments for the kinds of experiences (such as living with a colicky, inconsolable baby for five months) that most of her college colleagues could not relate to.

At the end of two years, Tashon was one of only five students from her original cohort of nearly 30 to complete the entire curriculum and qualify for a diploma. With her diploma in hand, she knew two things for sure. The first was that she really loved to write and the second was that she didn't want to get a job that would require her to commute every day and put her children in daycare. What she really wanted was to have a career as a writer and also to be a stay-at-home parent to her two preschool-aged sons.

As a single parent with no other means of income, it was a risky move, but Tashon decided being her own boss was the only option that would allow the kind of freedom and flexibility she needed. Having completed an internship with the Vancouver Board of Trade while working towards her writing diploma, Tashon approached the director of communications and proposed writing for the Board on a freelance basis. Working on assignments for several departments within the Board, it wasn't long before she started to build her client list and realize her dream of being a self-employed freelance writer.

More than a decade after making the decision to follow her dream, Tashon told me she is proud that she has been able to provide for her children (who are now entering their teens) while also having a career that she loves. Although she says there were a lot of sacrifices in the early years, she has no doubt that every one of them was worth it because she gets to live life on her own terms. Her advice to others: "You don't have to live your life the way other people expect you to. Discover what works for you and use your imagination to build the life you want."

—◊—

As I mentioned at the beginning of this chapter, it can take a great deal of effort to get a dream off the ground and some people (competitive athletes, artists, musicians, etc.) must dedicate years, perhaps even decades, to their dream before they reach the point where their dream really begins to happen. That kind of commitment is an inspiration for the rest of us, which reminds me of a story.

Cecil Green Park is the name of a magnificent old home on an equally magnificent property at the corner of Chancellor Boulevard and Marine Drive in the Point Grey area of Vancouver.

This beautiful house was magnanimously turned over to

THE POWER OF A DREAM

the University of British Columbia in 1967 and has subsequently been used for conferences, seminars and other public and private functions. Those directly connected with the university have first dibs for reservations, but with lots of lead time, it is available to the public for weddings, receptions and other celebrations.

My wife and I were privileged to attend a wedding at Cecil Green where John, a handsome groom, and Louise Voiles, a stunningly beautiful bride, exchanged vows in the estate's garden.

Following the ceremony, there was a champagne buffet in the Grand Hall, where we dined to the sounds of light classics played by a quartet — two violins, a cello and a large grand piano — everything was perfect.

During the course of the afternoon, I learned some wonderful things about the grand piano that Monica Pfau was playing and something of its history.

Ignacy Jan Paderewski was born in Poland in 1860 and in addition to becoming his country's first Prime Minister, he is also remembered as an internationally famous virtuoso pianist and composer. Paderewski played in the opening season of Carnegie Hall in 1891. In addition to playing in New York and many other cities, he once came to Vancouver.

As often happens with the best of pianists, Paderewski brought his grand piano with him. And in Vancouver, the last stop on the tour, after it had done yeoman concert service and been carried for many thousands of gruelling recital miles, the piano was put up for sale.

The buyer was the Marquess of Anglesey, who moved

it to the Thompson Valley area of British Columbia, about 200 miles northeast of Vancouver, to a place called Walhachin.

It was many years later that Vancouver's Dr. William Gibson initiated a drive to bring the Paderewski piano back to the city. Cecil Green Park was being refurbished in the mid-'60s and Gibson apparently coaxed or cajoled the residents of Walhachin to entrust the piano to the University of British Columbia.

They did; it was brought to the coast and remains today as an often used, wonderful piece of musical history in Cecil Green Park.

One of the famous stories about Paderewski relates to his visit to New York in 1891, where he ended up as a guest speaker at a polo club. Slightly confused, he is alleged to have said: "You are souls who play polo, and I am a Pole who plays solo!" Beverly Sills told the story on the PBS broadcast that celebrated Carnegie Hall's 100th anniversary.

Another story about the pianist tells of a young mother who had a dream and a wish that her young son might someday become a concert pianist. Unfortunately, her encouragement for him to practice, practice, practice fell on deaf ears.

'If only he could hear and see Paderewski play,' she thought. 'Perhaps it would inspire him.'

As fortune would have it, Paderewski came to town and the mother bought two tickets. On the evening of the recital, she dressed her son in his concert best and off they went to see the famous man play.

At the hall, distracted by the crowd and chatting with friends and neighbours, the mother didn't see her son heading off to the stage, drawn to the shining piano that stood waiting to be played.

He climbed onto the huge bench and began to peck out the chords of "Chopsticks," a tune that is familiar to anyone who has even been close to a piano.

"Who's the kid?" someone yelled. "Get him off the stage!"

"Who'd bring a kid here anyway?" someone else shouted.

In his dressing room, Paderewski heard the commotion and the music. He grabbed his coat and ran onto the stage. As he encouraged the boy to keep going, the Polish maestro engulfed him with his arms and improvised a spectacular accompaniment around the rhythm of the tune's simple chords.

As they finished, the crowd cheered and Paderewski and the boy proudly took their bows.

"Don't quit," whispered Paderewski. "Keep playing. Keep practicing. Be persistent."

I don't know whether or not that young boy ever made it to the concert stage. But I suspect that Paderewski's encouragement kept him going and opened the doors that night to a new world of musical appreciation. If nothing else at all had come from that chance encounter, it still would have been a great, great gift.

I thought about all these things at the wedding at Cecil Green Park — seeing the young couple take their vows in the midst of all that beauty, hearing the music and knowing a little more about the piano, its history and about the man who gave us the delicate and beautiful "Minuet in G" and left a piece of priceless history that would keep on making music for British Columbia and its visitors for many, many years.

I suspect that those of us who have never pursued a really big dream like becoming a world-famous pianist sometimes think our dreams are as insignificant as "Chopsticks" on a concert grand. That the world tours and the curtain calls are being taken more often than not by people other than us. We could think like that. Or we can think differently and hear Paderewski's encouraging words. Don't quit. Keep going. Don't give up.

When you come to Vancouver, and sooner or later everyone does, be sure to stop by Cecil Green Park. The folks there will make you very welcome. Ask to see the piano. And maybe when no one is looking, you might peck out the chords of "Chopsticks."

Chris Guillebeau talks about how his choice to become what he calls a "travel hacker" (someone who travels the globe without spending much money to do it) has meant that he had to make choices about what is important to him . . . he doesn't have a car or a house; instead he takes transit or rides his bike and rents an apartment so that he can spend his money on travel. He also doesn't have a "job," instead earning his income from products and services offered through his website and blog, *The Art of Non-Conformity*. A couple of years ago, Guillebeau decided to fulfill one of his big dreams, which is to visit every country in the world within a period of just a few years.

When Guillebeau (who calls Portland, Oregon, home) travels overseas, the people he meets are always fascinated by what he is doing and invariably make a comment such as, "That sounds amazing, I wish I could do that."

"What's keeping you from it?" is his standard response.

It's an excellent question and one we should all ask when we find ourselves wishing we had something different than what we have or making rationalizations for why we aren't living our dream.

Perhaps the most common rationalization for not taking action is one that I'm sure you're familiar with: "I don't have the money to pursue my dream."

Chances are if you live in North America or elsewhere in the developed world, you have more than enough money to meet your basic needs and quite a bit left over for the things that you want (and perhaps think that you need to survive), such as your own house or condo (complete with a big mortgage payment), a car (or two or three), a cellphone, cable television and high-speed Internet service, just to name a few recurring expenses that can add up very quickly. The truth is that beyond basic food, shelter and transportation, everything else that we choose to spend our money on is exactly that, a choice, our choice. Whether consciously or unconsciously, we choose what we value when we decide how to spend our time, money and other resources.

Are you willing to sacrifice your dream in order to continue to live the life you have or are you willing to sacrifice a few comforts and do what it takes in order to have your dream?

Here are two questions that Guillebeau suggests people ask themselves to help determine if they are on the right path to fulfilling their dreams:

1. Am I satisfied with my job or career? Is it meeting my needs and fulfilling my desires?

Your job should do more than simply provide income for the rest of your life. Ask yourself, what am I working for? Am I working to make a living or to make a life? If your work supports your goals, that's great. If it doesn't, maybe it's time to make a change.

2. What are my financial priorities?

If you have difficulty figuring this one out, there's an easy way to tell. Just look back at your bank statements, credit-card statements, expense records and receipts from the past six months. Whether you like it or not, where you've been spending a lot of money is where your priorities lie.

Once you fully understand what you want, it's not usually that difficult to get it.

Guillebeau's advice for dealing with critics and naysayers: "At all stages of life, people will gladly offer you unsolicited lists of things you 'must' do, be or have. Most of the time you can nod your head, walk away and ignore them."

For those who dream of travelling the world but still think a lot of money is required, he offers, "If you save two dollars a day for three years, you can go anywhere in the world. Most places will take much less than three years." And if you're willing to get creative, you can travel "hack" like Chris Guillebeau and others who manage to travel in style without spending a lot of money.

—∭—

Superlatives for the opening ceremonies of the 2010 Winter Olympic Games are many: awe-inspiring, spectacular, monumental.

Four out of five Canadians from coast to coast to coast watched these spectacular ceremonies, which ignited a patriotism that is rarely witnessed in this country. Flags were flown everywhere — from cars, bicycles, apartment buildings, boats, bridges, private homes and city hall. Downtown Vancouver was a sea of red and each afternoon and evening it reminded me of walking the streets of New York — there were so many people!

So, who created the opening and closing ceremonies? The multi-talented David Atkins produced both events, in addition to the evening victory/medal ceremonies at B.C. Place Stadium. Atkins is someone who likes to dream big.

The following excerpt is from the official Vancouver 2010.com website:

Atkins, who was the Executive Producer and Artistic

Director of the Sydney 2000 Summer Games Ceremonies as well as the Open and Closing Ceremonies of the 15th Asian Games in Doha in 2006, admits that working on the Olympic Games becomes a bit addictive.

"The pressure is quite extraordinary on every member of the team. These are once-only events. It's a highly charged experience with years of work coming down to one night, one time and one place."

In a breakfast meeting with Shel Piercy, associate producer of the 2010 Winter Olympic opening and closing ceremonies, he shared with me seven principles that David Atkins lives by.

David's Seven Rules:

1. For the Canadian Games, David had a staff of 190 men and women and he knew each one of them by name.

2. A true leader never asks any member of the team to do anything he wouldn't do.

3. David understands the pressure he is under, in that everything he produces must be world-class.

4. Every member of David's team attends every production meeting — no excuses. If a meeting is called and you have another appointment, then change it.

5. David is insistent that you must rehearse, rehearse, rehearse, then practice, practice, practice. How can a show be world-class if you don't rehearse and practice? It's impossible to give your best performance on the big day if you haven't put in the time.

6. Yes, it takes a huge financial investment, but David's entire team has made an emotional investment. Without this emotional investment, it just doesn't happen. As I've

said in the past, "Without an emotional attachment to a business idea or career, you will not pursue it with passion. If the idea or deal has not been properly thought through, success is not likely. You need to balance the two for success."

7. David doesn't want to hear what you can't do; he only wants to hear what you can do.

This is not bad advice no matter what your dream is. I wholeheartedly agree that you must rehearse, rehearse, rehearse and practice, practice, practice before you get really good at anything.

SOMETHING TO THINK ABOUT

Any dream is possible if we are willing to make the necessary commitment.

Leo Babauta, author of *Zen Habits*, reminds us that priorities are not what we say they are — they're what we actually do. It's one thing to set priorities, it's something else again to really live them. He also points out that one of the most common mistakes we make in setting priorities is to overcomplicate things or try to focus on too many things at once. The truth is that we can only focus on a couple of priorities at a time, so we need to be really clear on what they are.

Schedule some time each day to do something that supports your most important dream, whatever it might be, so that your life will actually reflect the priorities you set.

"I start where other men leave me."

— Thomas Edison

CHAPTER 6

JUMP AND THE NET WILL MATERIALIZE

We don't always have to plan every step of the way before we go after our dreams. If we take a leap of faith and put ourselves out there, we will find a way to get what we need to make things happen. It might not come about exactly as we expected, but that, I believe, is an important part of the adventure.

During the 2009 World Police and Fire Games, more athletes were in Vancouver than for the Olympics — 10,500 from 56 countries around the globe. Their families and friends joined them, boosting tourism in the province for several weeks and contributing an estimated $84 million to the economy. It was a remarkable event that introduced British Columbia to emergency personnel from around the globe.

Bringing the games to Vancouver took a leap of faith on the part of two people, Burnaby firefighters Jeff Clark and Miles Ritchie.

These two individuals were abroad at an international planning meeting for the games when it occurred to them that Vancouver would be the perfect place to host the event. Unable to contact the leadership in their department, they decided to submit the application anyway and posted the

$5,000 fee to their personal credit cards.

On the flight home they were hoping their wives would be supportive and their department would agree to host the games — and reimburse them.

The 2009 Games, which took place from July 31 to August 9, were a resounding success and the biggest ever hosted in the organization's 26-year history. They were also named Sport Event of the Year at the Prestige Awards held in Toronto as part of the Canadian Sport Tourism 2010 Congress.

Amazing things can happen when we're willing to put ourselves out into the world, take a chance and do what our gut tells us to do. Terry McBride, president and CEO of Nettwerk Music Group, is an excellent example.

"I have to say, I owe my success to not listening to the advice of others," explained McBride in a *BCBusiness* article about successful leaders. "The music business is very central to Toronto, Los Angeles, New York, Nashville and London. Vancouver is not really on the map, except for a couple of managers here.

"When we released our first three records, I went back east and started showing them around to all of these different players there. I was told I would never succeed if I stayed in Vancouver, but that just made us more determined to stick to our vision. If I was going to give any advice to someone, it would be, understand that all perspectives are right, but follow your own intuition, not that of others."

Cindy Lee of T&T Supermarkets is another entrepreneur who took a big leap of faith that paid off. When she first opened T&T Supermarkets in 1993, she admits she didn't have any management skills or supermarket know-how. In fact, she opened her first store to help her husband, who wanted to build President Plaza, an Asian shopping mall in Richmond, B.C., and needed a supermarket as a tenant.

In the beginning, Lee notes, the business was a disaster. Having opened two supermarkets one month apart, she had 200 employees and no experience. In the first six months, the company lost two-thirds of its capital and she worried constantly that it might go bankrupt. Unable to sleep, Lee turned to her father in tears, acknowledging that she couldn't handle the challenge and wanting to quit.

Being a wise man, her father encouraged her not to give up.

"Every new business is tough at first," he told her. "What you have to do is surround yourself with people who are better and smarter than you and then treat them well. Then they'll share their knowledge with you and follow you."

Following his advice, Lee hired professional managers to come in to help and was able to turn T&T around in one year.

Today, when Lee encounters a problem or challenge in her business, the first question she often asks herself is, "Who can help me, who can I talk to for advice and expertise?"

Michael Gates Gill, author of *How Starbucks Saved My Life*, is a great proponent of leaping with the faith that something good will happen. Nearing retirement, Gill lost everything that he thought was important in his life. A Yale-educated advertising executive making a six-figure salary, he was let go from his job (basically because they thought he was getting too old), saw his marriage disintegrate and was diagnosed with a brain tumour (I can't imagine that many of us would ever have to face so much all at once).

As the son of famous *New Yorker* writer Brendan Gill, during Michael's childhood years, the family's social circle had included the likes of Ernest Hemingway and Jacqueline Onassis. At the age of 63, desperate and without health insurance, Michael Gill found redemption and a new sense of purpose where he least expected it: working as a barista at Starbucks. His humble story, which was derived in large part from a journal he kept to help him make sense of what was happening to him as his life fell apart, became an instant best-seller and the movie rights have since been purchased by Tom Hanks.

Having accepted the job at Starbucks on a leap of faith (he walked into the store during a hiring event and was offered a job on the spot), with no expectation about where it might lead, Gill soon found himself feeling useful and happy for the first time in many years despite the fact that he was the one serving instead of the one being served.

With all of the trappings of his previous life gone, today Gill says he lives in a simple apartment that is close to his work and counts himself both lucky and blessed. At what he himself calls a late age, Gill says he learned from his new boss and colleagues (people he would never have taken the time to get to know in his old life) what really matters to him and he is thankful for what he calls his "fall from grace."

In an interview prior to his book tour for *How Starbucks Saved My Life*, Gill was asked what message he has for others who find themselves in difficult circumstances. He said that he really has two messages: "Be ready to be happily surprised in life and don't be afraid to make a fool of yourself."

He also has this advice for those who want to make their life better:

- Leap, with faith: Sometimes it pays to leap without looking and say yes without thinking (Gill accepted the Starbucks job immediately and completely on a whim).
- Let yourself be helped: Pride is even more paralyzing than fear.
- Look with respect at every individual you see: Sheltered in a privileged world, Gill was raised to avoid eye contact with those who were considered to be different from him. Now he realizes the potential in everyone who crosses his daily path.

—m—

It is important to find the support you need to change your life or achieve your dream and as Michael Gates Gill's example clearly shows, sometimes that support can come from an unlikely place. This next story, which appeared in my earlier book *If Only I'd Said That: Volume IV*, also reminds us that opportunity can present itself in many different ways and we shouldn't be so quick to dismiss people out of hand just because they don't appear to be who or what we are accustomed to:

One day, a woman, dressed in a faded gingham dress, and her husband, wearing a threadbare homespun suit, stepped off the train in Boston. They walked timidly — without an appointment — into the Harvard University president's office. The president's secretary took one look at them and told them the president would be busy all day.

"We'll wait," the wife replied.

For hours they waited, while the secretary hoped they would leave. But they didn't.

Finally, the secretary disturbed the president, telling him, "Maybe if you see them for a few minutes, they'll leave."

The president agreed, though he didn't have time, and hated such people cluttering the place.

When they were seated, the woman said, "We had a son who attended Harvard for one year. He loved it, but last year he was accidentally killed. My husband and I would like to erect a memorial to him somewhere on campus."

"Madam," the president replied, "we can't put up a statue for every person who attended Harvard. If we did, the university would look like a cemetery."

"Oh, no," the woman said. "Not a statue . . . a building."

"A building? Do you have any idea how much that costs? We have over $7.5 million invested in our buildings here."

The woman was silent for a moment, then turned to her husband and whispered, "Is that all it costs to build a university? Why don't we just start our own?"

Her husband nodded.

The president's face was a study in confusion as Mr. and Mrs. Stanford left the office.

Back in Palo Alto, California, the couple established Stanford University as a memorial to a son whom Harvard no longer cared about.

Well, looks can be deceiving and I'm sure the president of Harvard probably kicked himself later for this lost opportunity. On the positive side, the Stanfords' determination to build a monument to their son led to the establishment of a university that has provided educational opportunities to help fulfill the dreams of thousands of students.

The realization that we only get one life should motivate and inspire, but sometimes it has the opposite effect and it can scare us into inaction.

Whenever I need a reminder, I look at the following list, titled *How to Stay Young:*

    1. Throw out nonessential numbers. This includes age, weight and height. Let the doctors worry about

them. After all, that is what you pay them for.

2. Keep only cheerful friends. The grouches will only pull you down.

3. Keep learning. Learn more about the computer, hobbies, gardening, whatever. Never let your brain go idle for longer than it takes to recharge your batteries.

4. Enjoy the simple things.

5. Laugh, often, long and loud. Laugh until you gasp for breath.

6. The tears happen. Accept the losses that come your way, grieve them and move on. Life is about living.

7. Surround yourself with what you love, whether it's family, pets, keepsakes, music, plants or hobbies. Your home is your sanctuary.

8. Cherish your health. If it is good, preserve it. If it is unstable, improve it. If it is beyond what you can improve, get help.

9. Don't take guilt trips. Take a trip to the park, to the beach, or even to another country, but don't go where the guilt is. Guilt doesn't motivate; it sucks the life out of us.

10. Tell the people you love that you love them, at every opportunity. Trust me, no one ever tires of hearing those words if they are sincere.

We all need to live life to its fullest every day!

—m—

A return visit earlier this year and a stay at the history-rich Grosvenor House Hotel during a trip to London brought back some fond memories.

When my daughter Rebecca was in Grade 6, she had a dream of being fluent in English and French. For a Canadian kid, it was a pretty good dream. After all, Canada's two official languages are English and French.

Through primary school, junior and senior high, Rebecca was taught entirely in French and, through her good efforts, she became, and remains, bilingual. In fact, I remember that from quite early in her immersion, she conversed in French to her friends on the phone. My wife Kay and I, who remain unilingually rooted in English, didn't have a clue what she was talking about but we have always been happy to support her dreams.

During her first year at Simon Fraser University in Vancouver, Rebecca had the urge to continue her education and her French immersion in France. Together we chose a university in Nice with Canadian links. In the summer prior to her departure, she worked to help with the burden of what would be a substantially greater expense — certainly much more than an easy daily commute to Simon Fraser.

Even though we had always spent our holidays together as a family and had travelled all over the place, Rebecca had never lived away from home. There was no question that the flight to London and on to France, and the long time away from home that would follow, would be daunting.

In September 1994, I took her to the airport in Vancouver for the continuation of her life adventure. With just 25 minutes to go before the British Airways flight left for London, I said to Rebecca, "It's time, kiddo." I knew where the gate was, and how long it would take her to get through security and onto the plane.

She paused for a moment, then in front of everyone, dropped her knapsack, threw her arms around my neck and said: "Dad, I love you so much. I'm scared to death. I don't want to go!"

But she did go. Her dream was still happening.

A few weeks earlier, probably anticipating that the early stages of life in Nice would be anything but nice, Rebecca had convinced me to somehow arrange a speaking assignment or other business meeting in London around the end of November. It would be great, she said. I could fly her up from the south of France and we could spend a weekend together.

Being a sucker of a dad, but more so because I love her, I figured it would be a great idea. The lobby of the Grosvenor, I said. It's a promise.

At the time, I had absolutely no idea how I might get to London, but being perpetually positive and always believing that you really can do what you think about most of the time, I started to think of almost nothing else but how to get to London in late November, hopefully for the lowest cost, and ideally, at no cost.

Within a few weeks, I had secured a speaking engagement in the Bahamas, which would take place on the weekend prior to the projected London date. That assignment would be followed by an engagement in New York, just two days ahead of the London weekend. Hey, except for the Atlantic crossing, I was there.

I took the plunge and booked a ticket from New York

to London. Rebecca would fly from Nice, we would have a great weekend and I would keep my promise as a dad. Rebecca, of course, never doubted that it would happen.

Then I thought to myself: 'That was pretty easy. Now how can I make this thing even better?'

I had accumulated points on another airline, so I said to Kay and our other daughters Samantha and Amanda: "Why don't you take a few days off and fly to London to surprise the heck out of Rebecca?" They didn't take much convincing. After all, it's the spontaneous decisions that often provide the best family memories.

Part of our family's success is good communication and while everybody dearly wanted to go to London, Kay and Amanda were going into finals at university and reluctantly had to decline. So as it turned out, I would wing in from New York and Samantha would fly directly from Vancouver to London. We would meet at the Grosvenor a few hours before Rebecca arrived from Nice. What had started as a fun weekend would still go right over the top, despite having to leave Kay and Amanda to their exams.

But there would be more.

I arranged with Anna Ponur, the guest relations manager at the Grosvenor House on Park Lane, to have Samantha hidden behind the check-in counter. Just as Rebecca was signing in, she would leap out and shout: "Surprise!"

At 7:30 p.m. as Sam was preparing to get herself into position and I was pacing the Grosvenor House lobby, a cab pulled up at the front and out stepped Rebecca.

If the Vancouver airport departure in September had been one filled with sadness, this was a moment of pure happiness. They say that hearts leap and mine certainly did that night. We ran to greet each other, hugged hard and cried tears of joy.

We talked beside the cab. I told Rebecca that I had arranged for her to have her own room and that she would have to check in herself. We went inside and began to walk toward the registration desk.

Sam, meanwhile, was in the back room getting ready to play her role, and as she stood there waiting, the hotel manager walked into the room. Seeing Sam, an obvious stranger among the cash, the accounts receivable and other documents, he quite rightly asked who she was and what was she doing in the hotel's very private space?

At this point, guest relations manager Anna jumped in, explaining that the guy coming toward the counter was the "intruder's" father and the girl next to him was the "intruder's" sister. The father was from Vancouver, the sister was from Nice, they hadn't seen each other for a while and what was about to happen would end in a delightful family reunion. A bright guy, the manager picked up on the scheme in a second.

Turning to one of the hotel employees, he asked her to slip out of her Grosvenor House uniform jacket and pill-box hat and give them to Sam. The event was beginning to have all the elements of a French farce, mixed nicely with a ridiculous British edge.

Sam, now in Grosvenor uniform, bow tie and hat, walked calmly to the desk as Rebecca, head down, was signing in.

"May I have your passport, please?" said Sam in a finely

concocted British accent.

Rebecca looked up, fumbled for her passport, looked up, fumbled again, then realized in a spectacular instant that the pillbox-hatted person behind the counter was her sister Samantha.

The small crowd that had now gathered and was onto the act cheered wildly as the Legge family threesome came together in a hug. As we walked away to the tea room, I saw two men, a woman and guest relations manager Anna wiping tears from their eyes. Magic times can happen anywhere.

Shortly after our reunion in London, I received the following note from Rebecca:

I'm not sure where to begin when I think of the incredible things that you have done for me. Being away for such a long time has shown me how much I appreciate you not only as a father, but as a friend. Your constant love and support have helped to keep me strong and my spirits high. Not a day goes by that I don't think about the way you make me laugh and smile. I miss so many things that I hadn't realized were so important to me — your cheerful disposition, your words of wisdom, your unconditional love. You are the most amazing father and I couldn't ask for anything more.

Thank you for everything.

I love you,

Bec

Success is sweeter when shared with a loving family . . . a family like mine. It's important to support the dreams of those we love and to give them the freedom to pursue those dreams.

Whether we realize it or not, we also support the dreams of people we have never even met.

In one of my previous books, I told the story of Charles Plumb, who is a member of the Speakers Roundtable organization and a dear friend and colleague. He was once a U.S. Navy jet pilot in Vietnam. After 75 combat missions, his plane was destroyed by a surface-to-air missile. Plumb ejected and parachuted into enemy hands.

He was captured and spent six years in a communist prison in Vietnam. He survived the ordeal and today lectures on lessons learned from that experience.

One day, when Plumb and his wife were sitting in a restaurant, a man at another table came up and said, "You're Plumb! You flew jet fighters in Vietnam from the aircraft carrier *Kitty Hawk*. You were shot down!"

"How in the world did you know that?" asked a very surprised Plumb.

"I packed your parachute," the man replied.

Plumb gasped in surprise and gratitude.

The man pumped his hand and said, "I guess it worked!"

Plumb assured him, "It sure did. If your chute hadn't worked, I wouldn't be here today."

Plumb couldn't get to sleep that night, thinking about the man who had packed his parachute.

"I kept wondering what he had looked like in a Navy uniform," he says. "A white hat, a bib in the back and bell-bottom trousers.

"I wonder how many times I might have seen him and not even said, 'Good morning, how are you?' or anything at all because, you see, I was a fighter pilot and he was just a sailor."

Plumb reflected on the many hours the sailor must have spent at a long wooden table in the bowels of the ship, carefully weaving the shrouds and folding the silks of each chute, holding in his hands each time, the fate of someone he didn't even know.

Now, when Plumb speaks to an audience, he always asks them, "Who's packing your parachute?"

Everyone has someone who provides what they need to make it through the day.

Plumb also points out that he needed many kinds of parachutes when his plane was shot down over enemy territory — he needed his physical parachute, his mental parachute, his emotional parachute and his spiritual parachute. He called on all of these supports before reaching safety.

Sometimes in the daily challenges that life gives us, we miss what is really important, such as when we fail to say hello, please or thank you, congratulate someone on something wonderful that has happened to them, give a compliment, or just do something nice for no reason. As you continue on your path, take time to recognize the contribution that others make to your success and be thankful for the people who pack your parachutes.

Sometimes the best way to achieve our dreams is by helping others to achieve theirs. No matter what work you choose to do in life, do it with care and take pride in knowing that you are supporting the success of others.

—m—

I have a confession: I loved my years at Lester Pearson High School in New Westminster, B.C., 1957 to 1960. I never had so much fun in all my life: sock hops, school assemblies (where I first learned to speak as emcee at most assemblies), sweater clubs and Ivy League clothes. We all went to Pops Restaurant on Sixth Street after school and enjoyed milkshakes, sodas, hamburgers and fries; the place was so popular, we would have to fight for a seat.

The hit TV series *Happy Days*, which first aired in 1974 with the opening song performed by Bill Haley and his Comets, did a pretty good job of depicting the great high school years of the '60s.

My high school was named after Canada's 14th Prime Minister, the Honourable Lester Mike Pearson, who visited the school several times. He was past president of the United Nations General Assembly and a Nobel Prize winner.

This past May 1, we celebrated our 50th high school reunion. We had a smashing turnout of 178 "kids" (of course, today we are all in our mid to late 60s). We barely recognized past boyfriends, girlfriends or basketball and football teammates. Even with band members and close schoolmates, we had great difficulty remembering each other's names. We even struggled to distinguish the teachers from the students, but nothing was going to stop us from reconnecting with each other and reliving our "Happy Days" memories.

Our school principal was a man named Ian Douglas — a tough disciplinarian! We had an opportunity to reread his graduates' message of 1960.

"Do not shun the storms of life as you go off to seek your fortune," the message began. Following that, Principal Douglas related "The Parable of the Poplars." It goes like this:

In a corner of the Orphanage grounds there is a beautiful stand of tall silver poplars. You must have seen them because you walk past them every day. They were planted there by the Kiwanis Club when its members landscaped the grounds 30 years ago.

There are six poplars in the group. Five of them mark the corners of a regular pentagon; the sixth is growing in the centre. They have grown well — slim and clean — all except one. It is not so tall as the others, which are almost equal in height and health, and it is thinner with fewer leaves than the other poplar trees.

At this point in the parable I should say, "Which think ye is the poorest of the poplars?" but I suppose that you are way ahead of me and guess that the answer to my poor parable is, "The tree in the centre." And that is the end of my story. But I suggest that the next time you pass those poplars you lean over the fence and observe the irony in the tree that has been sheltered from all the storms and common assaults of the last 30 years and yet has grown less tall and less handsome than the trees that protected it.

— Ian Douglas

The strongest tree in the forest is not the one protected from the storm and hidden from the sun, but the one that stands in the open where it is compelled to struggle for its existence against the winds and rains and scorching sun.

Struggle and resistance develop strength. Use this to aid you in your struggles for success. If you're anything like me, I've grown the most and learned life's lessons the best when faced with struggles and resistance — it's part of life. So never give up — or give in. Welcome these times as growing experiences and you'll be better for it.

(If you're curious to see the poplars yourself, the Orphanage is located behind the school on the corner of 6th and 8th Avenue in New Westminster, British Columbia.)

SOMETHING TO THINK ABOUT

My friend, author and speaker Brian Tracy, says, "You are a living magnet. What you attract into your life is in harmony with your dominant thoughts."

Never underestimate the power of belief. What we think is possible pretty much defines what is in fact possible and it is a principle that is in effect every moment of your life, so you must make sure that the majority of your thoughts are aimed at moving you closer to your dream. If you've been feeling controlled or restricted by your circumstances or you've felt a lack of motivation and direction — remember that all you need to overcome any situation or obstacle is within your power if you believe that it is.

This isn't magic and it certainly isn't a secret. The fact is that if we look for opportunities and solutions, we are more likely to be open to all of the possibilities that come our way and also to allow others to help us and even ask for help when we need it. Either way, eventually we find what we are looking for. It is time to give yourself permission — to dream, to aspire, to hope for the best and to reach for it. Believe that good things are on their way to you now and you'll soon see that they are.

Here's a little poem to help you remember that anything is possible if you're willing to take a leap of faith.

It Couldn't Be Done

Somebody said that it couldn't be done
But he with a chuckle replied
That "maybe it couldn't" but he would be one
Who wouldn't say so till he tried.
So he buckled right in with the trace of a grin
On his face. If he worried he hid it.
He started tossing as he tackled the thing
That couldn't be done, and he did it
Somebody scoffed: "Oh, you'll never do that
At least no one ever had done it;"
But he took off his coat and he took off his hat
And the first thing we knew he'd begun it.
With a lift of his chin and a bit of a grin,
Without any doubting or quiddit,
He started to sing as he tackled the thing
That couldn't be done, and he did it.
There are thousands to tell you it cannot be done,
There are thousands to prophesy failure,
There are thousands to point out to you one by one,
The dangers that wait to assail you.

But just buckle in with a bit of a grin,
Just take off your coat and go to it;
Just start in to sing as you tackle the thing
That "cannot be done," and you'll do it.
— Edgar A. Guest (1881-1959)

CHAPTER 7

MAKE ALTERATIONS AS REQUIRED

Sometimes reality gets in the way of our dreams. We can't be a *Canadian Idol* if we don't have the ability to sing and we'll never be a golf prodigy if we can't hit the ball. Sometimes we need to modify our dreams to fit our abilities, but that doesn't mean that we have to give up on those dreams.

Deborra Hope is a well-known media personality in British Columbia, a long-time journalist, news anchor and producer for the Global Television Network. She has been hosting the *Early News* and the "Insight" segment on the *News Hour* since 2001.

More than anything, Hope loves to tell a good story, but she also has another passion: a lifelong love of singing. She sings beautifully, by the way, enough so that she could have been a professional singer. Now, if you're wondering if Hope gave up on her dream of singing in the name of practicality, the answer is no. Instead, she found a way to pursue both of her dreams in a realistic way. During the week, she is a professional journalist and on evenings and weekends she sings with the West Coast Harmony Chorus and with Over the Moon, an award-winning quartet that offers a mix of jazz, swing and barbershop musical entertainment.

It is up to each one of us to determine how our dreams

will be realized. The important thing is to use the talents we have, take advantage of the opportunities that come our way and be flexible enough to make adjustments as needed. Without flexibility, many wonderful opportunities can pass us by. Here's a perfect case in point, which you may recall from the latest volume in my book series *If Only I'd Said That*:

Matt Harrington was a right-handed pitcher with a 95-plus-mph fastball. He was considered one of the top pitching prospects in the 2000 Major League Baseball draft. He was selected seventh overall by the Colorado Rockies. His agent asked for $4.9 million plus a signing bonus. The Rockies' final offer was $4 million and a guaranteed major league call-up. Harrington turned down the deal and sat out the season.

In the 2001 draft, Harrington slipped into the second round and was drafted by the San Diego Padres. He was the 58th overall pick. The Padres offered him a $1.2-million signing bonus, but he wanted twice that amount. Harrington rejected the offer and again declined to sign. That year he played in the minors.

In 2002, he was in the 13th round and the 374th overall pick. Harrington was drafted this time by the Tampa Bay Devil Rays. Again, he failed to agree to a contract. Tampa Bay offered him between $5,000 and $20,000. He didn't sign and played once again in the minor leagues.

In 2003, he was the 711th overall pick in the 24th round, and the Cincinnati Reds were offering him little more than simply a chance to play. Again he played in the minor leagues.

In 2004, he was drafted by the Yankees in the 36th round, 1089th overall. They didn't even bother to offer him a contract.

In 2005, Harrington became a free agent, allowing him to sign with any organized baseball team. Nobody signed him, and he played in the minors.

On October 10, 2006, he signed a minor league contract with the Chicago Cubs. He received no signing bonus but attended their spring training camp in hopes of signing a position. They released him.

This is the sad, sad story of a talented young pitcher who slipped further down the draft board each year and is considered today a very long shot ever to reach the major leagues.

So what's the lesson?

Is the lesson greed?

Is the lesson arrogance?

Is the lesson thinking you're too good?

Is the lesson selfishness?

Is the lesson stupidity?

At some point in your career, you need to move up from the minors to the majors. Perhaps this talented young pitcher needed to learn a valuable lesson: "Do more than you're paid to do, then pretty soon you will be paid to do what you do."

Matt Harrington never did make it to the majors. He still plays in the independent minor league baseball division.

—ᴍ—

We all have within us the seeds of greatness, but those seeds can only grow if we take the right action. Sometimes settling for a little less in order to achieve greater gains in the future might be necessary.

Last summer, Kay and I went on a cruise on the *Queen Mary II*. At dinner with the captain, I asked him, "If you needed to, how long would it take for you to stop this ship?"

"If I shut all the engines down it would take me about a mile to completely stop," he explained.

When we have a dream, we often want things to happen right away and become impatient when our plans don't unfold as we had imagined. However, just as with the cruise ship, it can take time to stop and then change direction.

Too often, we are more invested in the process than we need to be. Sometimes it is much better to focus on results and not worry about how we get there because there is almost always more than one way to make a dream come true. Often in my life, if I've wanted something that I couldn't get with the resources at hand, I've found another way.

When I was younger and living in London doing a television show, although I was living my dream, I wasn't making enough money to pay the bills. Instead of giving up or considering myself a failure, I did other things to make ends meet, like working in a clothing store and doing interviews for CBC Radio.

And even if you do fail, rather than beating yourself up over the failure of whatever it was that you undertook, think about all that you learned from the experience and use that knowledge to get yourself that much further in your next attempt.

If you want to live your dreams, you've got to make yourself better, you've got to have the courage to step out and do it, to commit with all you've got. When I was the Vancouver Board of Trade chair, I set out to be the best chair ever. I committed to go to every single board meeting, chair every event that I could and learn all I could from those who had held the position before me. As a result, I got the equivalent of an MBA in a year.

Looking back, however, I remember when I was originally approached to take on the position, I thought there was no possible way I could do it. But then Kay reminded me, "They wouldn't have asked you if they didn't think you could do it and if they believe you can do it, then maybe you can." So I jumped. I learned how to conduct meetings, I studied up on the policy issues that were pertinent to our members, I sought out the counsel of previous chairs, including my immediate predecessor, Graham Stamp, who told me, "I will be there to help you," and he was (at every meeting). It was a busy and challenging year for me. I learned how to run an organization effectively, but even more importantly, I learned that I was capable of so much more than I had imagined. I ended my year energized and excited, looking for new dreams to explore.

—⟋𝔪⟍—

Sometimes, the challenges we face can seem insurmountable, but as comic David Granirer has learned, that old saw about "where there's a will, there's a way," is actually true. In a profile in *The National Post*, the founder of Stand Up for Mental Health shared his philosophy. "Life is really all about realizing that possibilities don't always present themselves in the way you think they should," explained Granirer. "But if you're listening, and you're awake enough to the opportunities, you can find them in a lot of places."

Granirer doesn't just preach his theory, he lives it and that is how he became a professional counsellor, stand-up comedian and mental-health advocate.

Always the class clown at school, at age 16 Granirer began to experience depression and suicidal thoughts and eventually landed in the psychiatric ward where he stayed for six weeks. That experience led him to volunteer at the Crisis Intervention and Suicide Prevention Centre of British Columbia where he was able to help others who were going through much the same ordeal, and eventually he was hired to train new volunteers.

In 1991, Granirer became a qualified counsellor and opened his own practice but he never lost his love for comedy and entertaining those around him. One day he decided to try his hand at a stand-up comedy club on amateur night. Despite totally bombing on his first attempt, he realized that he was onto something and took a course in stand-up to learn the basics. Hearing the laughter of family and friends as he took the stage to perform at the class showcase at the end of the program, he knew he was hooked.

In addition to performing at clubs and comedy shows, he began teaching stand-up at Langara College in Vancouver, where he made an amazing important discovery that led him to a brilliant idea. Watching students who had suffered from anxiety, depression, chronic shyness and phobias suddenly blossom on stage, he realized that stand-up comedy was both therapeutic and empowering.

"There's something incredibly healing about telling a roomful of people exactly who you are and having them laugh and cheer," he says.

Realizing the potential of humour to heal, Granirer founded a new program called Stand Up for Mental Health, which teaches stand-up comedy to people dealing with depression, bipolar disorder, schizophrenia, obsessive-compulsive disorder, post-traumatic stress, drug addiction or even brain injury. At the end of each program, the students have the opportunity to perform before a live audience and many go on to perform at fundraising comedy events that bring in money to keep the program going.

Since it began in 2004, Stand Up for Mental Health has been featured in hundreds of media stories throughout the world. The coverage has helped to change public perception of mental-health challenges and fight the stigma around mental illness that leads to prejudice and discrimination.

"When you have a mental illness, one of the worst parts is the shame that goes along with it, and your life is full of incidents and stories and things that happen to you that were bad and you're ashamed of," explained Granirer in *The National Post* article.

To date, Stand Up for Mental Health has partnered with mental-health organizations to develop programs across Canada and in the United States. Some of the students from the program have been featured in a Global TV documentary called *Laughing Through the Pain* and in the award-winning documentary *Cracking Up*.

For David Granirer, running the program is a way to change hearts and minds, one laugh at a time, and the opportunity to live a dream that transforms people's lives. For the rest of us, his example is a lesson in how we can take whatever life throws at us, even something as potentially devastating as a serious mental illness, and turn it into a wonderful opportunity.

Optimism — whether it comes naturally or is learned — is good for you. Not only do happy people live longer than those who are pessimistic and cynical, but they also lead healthier lives. Researchers at the Mayo Clinic reviewed the records of people who completed the *Minnesota Multiphasic Personality Inventory* in the early 1960s. Three decades later, they found that pessimists, as compared to optimists, had an increased risk of death. The more pessimistic the personality, the greater the risk. In a follow-up study, it was found that optimistic people had better general health across the board.

If you're not naturally a glass half-full kind of person, you may still be able to learn to be more optimistic — and improve your health. Here are some suggestions for becoming more optimistic:

1. Stop negative self-talk. When you catch yourself thinking that you won't enjoy an event or do well on a project, stop the thought right in its tracks and turn it around. Instead, focus on identifying the positives in the situation (find at least one or two, even if they are small).

2. If you're irritated with your spouse, partner, child or other family member, think back to the last time the two of you shared a laugh or a special moment and how close it made you feel to them. Remind yourself of why they are important in your life.

3. Find joy in your work. No matter what kind of job you have, find some aspect that's personally satisfying and focus on that.

4. Surround yourself with positive, upbeat people and make sure you return the favour.

5. Deal with the situations that you can control and try to accept (or at least not worry about) those you can't. Letting go is a great stress reliever.

6. Put things in perspective. Life may take you on difficult paths, so try to find the adventure. A bump in the road is only temporary unless you choose to dwell on it.

7. Each day, write down three positive things that happened that day as well as a reason why you think those good things happened. This will help to keep you focused

on what is working in your life.

For me, one of the best ways to stay optimistic is to move my focus away from my own situation (and any negative thoughts, fears or anxieties that may be plaguing me) and instead focus on helping others. It's something I learned a number of years ago when my wife and I visited Israel together with some other folks from our church. A very rich cultural and spiritual journey indeed, the Holy Land offered some simple yet profound lessons on life.

For instance, the Dead Sea is dead because water flows *into* it, but nothing flows *out* of it. Brackish and stagnant, it is a gigantic collecting point where everything comes to a salty stop. The Sea of Galilee, however, which is situated in the same part of the world, is very much alive. Water comes in and water goes out. It is cleansed, aerated and supporting of life — of fish, of birds, and of people who are much more interested in the environment of that sea.

Human behaviour often mimics these two bodies of water. For example, we can cause things — including money — to flow into our lives and we can build fortunes and bless ourselves with all the trappings that financial wealth afford. In doing so, however, we don't necessarily provide enrichment to others or to the environment around us.

We end up like King Midas, who lost himself and his daughter with his wish for gold. We end up like the Dead Sea, stagnant in many respects, salty and crusty around the edges.

Life is enriched when wealth flows in and wealth and talent flow out. All my life I have attempted to save 10 per cent of everything I make for the life I hope to live tomorrow. We all need financial security and that's why I would recommend that the saving habit start as soon as possible for each of us.

With equal dedication, I have attempted to give away 10 per cent of everything I make. It may sound like a lot, but I have discovered time and time again that this action has never failed to bless me richly in all kinds of tangible ways.

My father always encouraged me to spend a considerable amount of time working with community organizations, and helping them achieve their goals and dreams. He once said to me, "Give back more to the community than you take out."

Like the Sea of Galilee, we can take it in, but we are made that much better when it flows through.

One of the things I like most about the Olympics is getting to see and hear all of the inspiring stories about athletes and their dreams. I was fortunate to meet a number of athletes during the 2010 Winter Games in Vancouver and one thing I noticed is that there is a special kind of energy around those who are so passionate about what they are doing. There are a multitude of lessons that we can learn from these athletes, but here are just a few that I think can be applied by anyone who needs a little extra inspiration to keep their dream on track.

1. You don't become the best at anything by blaming.
What you criticize you draw out of your life. Any competitive athlete knows that there are two ways to deal with a less-than-perfect performance. You can either focus on laying blame (on the weather, the field, the referee, the coach, the competition) or you can take responsibility for the result and learn from the experience. In life, as in sports, there are many times when things don't turn out as we intended. Either something goes wrong or the results just don't measure up to our expectations. That's when you need to look at what happened, determine what you can learn from the experience and then apply those lessons and make adjustments to your plan.

2. There's no substitute for hard work.
It took Canada's Alex Bilodeau just 29 seconds to win gold in the men's moguls at the 2010 Winter Olympics. Impressive for sure, but what's more impressive is what we didn't see. Alex, who is 22 years old, has been skiing since the age of two and training competitively for more than eight years. He learned his sport one skill at a time. He has suffered injuries and pain. He has also worked with sports psychologists to sharpen his competitive edge. It is important to realize that years of blood, sweat and tears went into a gold-medal performance that lasted less than 30 seconds. Far too often in life, we expect immediate gratification when the truth is that the real secret to success is old-fashioned hard work.

3. Those who succeed give it their all.

For athletes, the moment of truth is usually just that, one moment in time where they have to lay everything on the line. A half-hearted effort gets half-hearted results and that's just not good enough. If you really want to achieve your dream, you've got to believe it with every ounce of your being and be willing to put everything you've got into your performance (whatever that might be).

4. You can't let obstacles stop you from achieving your dream.

At some point or other, almost every athlete will experience a serious injury or setback that threatens their competitive career, but that doesn't stop them from getting back on their feet and trying again. Personal circumstances often cause us to change or delay our plans, but that doesn't mean we have to give up on our dreams. Size up the obstacle, brainstorm some ideas to deal with it, get help if you need to and then make a plan to get back on track and into the game.

5. If you plan to succeed, you can't fear failure.

Do you know of any athlete who has made it to the top without ever losing a competition? Not likely. So why do so many people expect to achieve their dreams without experiencing a few disappointments, failures or setbacks along the way? Failure is a by-product of trying. It's also a guidepost to success.

6. There's no need to go it alone.
Perhaps the most important lesson we can learn from competitive athletes is that going after your dream is easier when you are surrounded by people who support what you are doing (coaches, mentors, trainers, fans, benefactors, sponsors, etc). Your dream needs other people to help bring it to life — find the people who will support your dream.

SOMETHING TO THINK ABOUT
We often find it easier to focus on our flaws than we do on our talents. But what if our flaws are the very things that have given us our talents? Consider this timeless parable, which I featured in an early volume of *If Only I'd Said That*:

An old woman had two pots that she used to carry water from the stream to her small cottage. One of the pots had a crack in it, while the other was perfect and always de-livered a full portion of water. At the end of the long walk from the stream to the house, the cracked pot arrived only half full.

For two years, this went on daily, with the woman bringing home only one-and-a-half pots of water. Of course, the perfect pot was proud of its accomplishments. But the poor cracked pot was ashamed of its own imperfection, and miserable that it could only do half of what it had been made to do.

After two years of what it perceived to be bitter failure, it spoke to the woman one day by the stream. "I am ashamed of myself, because this crack in my side causes water to leak out all the way back to your house."

The old woman smiled, "Did you notice that there are flowers on your side of the path, but not on the other pot's side? That's because I have always known about your flaw, so I planted flower seeds on your side of the path, and every day while we walk back, you water them.

"For two years, I have been able to pick these beautiful flowers to decorate the table. Without you being just the way you are, there would not be this beauty to grace the house."

Each of us has our own unique flaw. But it's the cracks and flaws that make our lives so very interesting and rewarding. You've just got to take each peculiarity and make the most of it.

"There is but one cause of human failure and that is man's lack of faith in his true self."

— William James

CHAPTER 8

NEVER TOO LATE TO PURSUE YOUR DREAM

We can always find excuses why we shouldn't take the leap and go for it, but many inspiring people have proved that there is no expiry date on a dream.

Earl Nightingale once said, "Never give up on a dream because of time. The time will pass anyway."

My wife Kay and I have always felt blessed by the fact that she was able to be a stay-at-home mom and provide the stability, attention and guidance our three daughters required as they were growing up. But we both also knew that Kay had other dreams in addition to seeing our daughters become thriving young women.

When our children were young, Kay attended various parenting programs to help her meet the many challenges that are part and parcel of raising children. She also found that she enjoyed reading self-help books and sharing what she learned with others who were looking for guidance. As her interest grew, she took a number of counselling programs within the community to learn more and was eventually offered an opportunity to counsel at our church.

Discovering something that she was really good at and getting paid to do it was an incredible boost for Kay. It was something of her own and she relished the satisfaction that came from helping others. At the same time, she wanted to continue to develop her skills and perhaps get college credit towards a degree.

After learning about a three-year course called Caretakers that was being offered through another church that was trying to get accreditation for its programs, Kay signed on and completed the full three years only to learn that accreditation had not been granted and none of the courses would count for college credit.

Contemplating her options — give up on her dream of being a qualified counsellor, or go for it and actually enrol in university — Kay was hit full force with a huge fear of failure. In order to become a fully credited counsellor, she would need a master's degree, which would require upgrading her high school courses (she had been educated in England and had her O levels) and then at least six years of university to complete her bachelor's and then her master's. At 43 years of age, she would be almost 50 by the time she graduated. She struggled with her fear — could she do it? What if she tried and failed?

"You're going to be 50 whether you do it or not," I reminded her (although I'm not sure that's what she wanted to hear).

What eventually clinched it for Kay was when listening to Robert Schuller one day, she heard him say, "It is better to try at something and fail than to try at nothing and succeed."

She decided then and there, "It's worth a try. Whether or not I succeed and go the whole way, I have to try, to prove to myself that I can do it."

Once she had made up her mind, Kay never looked back. She began by upgrading her English and other prerequisites to get into college and decided on a bachelor's degree in religious education, which meant that she would have to take some theology courses as well.

It took her a year to complete all of the prerequisites and then she enrolled at Northwest Baptist Theological College in Langley to work on her bachelor's degree. Although her theological courses were at Northwest, she took her science and psychology courses at Trinity University where she eventually completed her master's of counselling as well.

Kay started her undergraduate degree in 1991 and graduated in 1998 with her master's. Our kids were amazing and supportive from the very beginning. At the time, Amanda was in Grade 7 and Rebecca was in Grade 9. Samantha, who is the oldest, was already in college, but all three of them rose to the challenge and helped out. They taught Kay how to use the computer and Samantha organized everyone to take turns making dinner during the week so Kay could focus on her assignments. They made up a calendar, where they each took a turn cooking and I got Friday night, which was easy because I either ordered something in or took everyone out to a restaurant for a treat. Kay took over the cooking on the weekends, which was family time and the only real break that she had from her studies. Friends and other interests were put on the back burner while she put all her energy into her dream.

Not only was Kay fulfilling her dream, she was becoming more confident and sure of her direction with every accomplishment along the way. "It's amazing, when you're motivated, you can do anything," she told me. "I feel as if God is saying to me, this is the path you need to take, and everything is just coming together."

It's good for all of us to face our fears and I could see that whatever fears Kay might have had about going back to school and getting her degree, she had looked them in the face and conquered them. A book that she says really helped her in doing so is called *Feel the Fear and Do It Anyway* by Susan Jeffers.

Following graduation, Kay was happy to be offered a position with the New Life Christian Counselling Clinic, which is where she completed one of her internships while at university. For the most part, her practice focuses on individual and marriage counselling, where she helps people who are struggling with issues such as depression, low self-esteem or anger management. Kay also continues to do premarital and private counselling at our church, which is something that is very rewarding for her.

When I mentioned to Kay that I wanted to include her story in this book, I asked her what she had learned from the experience that she would like to share with others. Here's what she told me: "It's never too late. If you have a dream inside of you and you know that you want to do it, you have to do it. Fulfilling your dream changes you; it grows you regardless of what you do with it. I learned so many other things about myself along the way and I would give anyone the same advice that led me to pursue my degree: it's never too late to try, so get going and go after your goals and your dreams."

—⁓—

A number of years ago, I came across a little story that had a significant impact on my life. I wish I could remember the speaker or author to give them their due credit, but my own files and research came up short on this point. Nevertheless, my recent book, *If Only I'd Said That: Volume V*, had its genesis in that story and I would like to share it with you again here.

In truth, it's a very simple story, or parable to be more precise, but one that truly could impact how you respond to all of the opportunities — big and small — that present themselves in your life every day:

Many years ago, a young man found himself walking along a deserted pebble beach. All alone, with just the knapsack on his back, he stopped to look out over the water, contemplating life and his future.

Suddenly, a genie appeared and told the young man to empty his knapsack and fill it up with as many pebbles as he could.

"If you do this, tomorrow morning you will be both happy and sad," said the genie, before disappearing as suddenly as he had arrived.

Despite his utter amazement, the young man dutifully did what the genie had told him to do.

The next morning when he awoke and looked into his knapsack, he was astonished to find that all of the pebbles had turned into diamonds. And just as the genie had predicted, he felt both happy and sad.

Happy that such a magical thing was possible and sad because he wished now that he'd taken the time to pick up even more pebbles.

What pebbles have you left on the beach of your life that might have turned into diamonds?

Perhaps they were:

- Ideas that you never acted upon
- Educational opportunities that you allowed to pass by
- Friends you could have made or kept
- Great business ideas that you didn't follow through with
- Children you could have spent more time with
- Relationships that might have been more meaningful
- An unfinished or unpublished book that you could have shared with the world
- Opportunities to participate in your community and enrich the lives of others

Or, perhaps something else that you let slip away?

Remember these questions from Chapter 5:

- How much am I willing to pay for my dream?
- How soon am I willing to pay it?
- How will I handle criticism?
- How will I overcome my fears?
- How hard am I willing to work?

Too often, we don't think we have the time to stop and ask ourselves the important questions, never mind the time it would take to answer those questions. Giving priority to our everyday responsibilities, such as earning a living, raising children and paying the mortgage, our dreams are pushed to the back of the closet where, more often than not, they wither and die.

But dreams don't have to die and they don't have to wait. With all of the educational opportunities now available and the flexibility offered by so many colleges, universities, technical and art schools, for people who have a dream that requires some sort of study, there's no time like the present to get started. Even if you just take one course at a time or study online through a distance education program, every step forward is another step closer to your dream and you don't have to sacrifice your family or your job to do it.

Elpi Lagouros, who was featured recently in a *National Post* article on dreams, did it. A mother of two, she had always had two passions. The first was teaching, which she pursued as her profession, and the second was interior decorating.

It took turning 40 for her to realize that if she ever wanted to realize her second dream, she was going to have to take some sort of action. Not only did she want to prove to herself that she could do it, she also wanted to be a good role model for her children, to show them that you should never give up on your dream.

With a full-time job and two young teenagers at home, Lagouros knew she wouldn't be able to enrol in the full-time, 15-course program that would give her an interior decorating certificate. Realistically, she would only be able to take two courses a year (which meant that it would take quite a few years to finish), but that didn't deter her or slow her down.

Emboldened by the support of her family, Lagouros embarked on her dream and was soon juggling two nights a week at college, in addition to running the kids to activities and taking care of her other responsibilities. It took organization and discipline to find the time to complete her assignments for the course, but she put every ounce of effort she had into doing the best she could on each project.

As with every dream, Lagouros had to make sacrifices to make it happen. During the six years that it took to complete her certificate in interior decorating, all of her leisure time was spent doing homework and completing assignments — still, she has no regrets. She cried with joy the day she finished her last course at college and was even more overjoyed when her Grade 5 class gave her a card congratulating her and telling her how proud they were on her graduation.

Although she has no plans at present to give up her career as a teacher to take up interior decorating as a career, Elpi Lagouros proved to herself that she can do anything she puts her mind to.

—◊—

A dream is an inspiring picture of the future that energizes your mind, your will and your emotions, empowering you to do everything you can to achieve it. Henry David Thoreau once said: "The mass of men lead lives of quiet desperation."

You may succeed if nobody else believes in you, but you will never succeed if you don't believe in yourself.

Our deepest fear is not that we are inadequate — it is that we are powerful beyond measure. Very often, we ask ourselves, "Who am I to be brilliant, gorgeous, talented and fabulous?"

Actually, who are you not to be?

We were born to make manifest the glory of God that is within us.

I believe that when we meet our maker, the first question isn't going to be about how well we stuck to the rules . . . oh, that will come sooner than later. The first question will be, "Why didn't you become all that you could be and use all of the talents that were given you?"

Reaching your God-given potential requires taking responsibility for yourself and your life; it means taking a leadership role with yourself.

So, what is leadership? Leadership is all about influence. And the first person you need to influence is yourself. So many of us keep worrying about what other people think of our dreams and so we get stopped right in our tracks.

Do you know the 18/40/60 rule by John Maxwell?

When you're 18, you worry what everybody is thinking about you.

When you're 40, you don't really care what anybody thinks of you.

And when you are 60, you realize that nobody has

been thinking about you all along, they've been too busy worrying about their own concerns.

So . . .

Grab hold of your dream and go for it! Dreams have enormous power and as Nido Qubein so rightly points out, "Your present circumstances don't determine where you can go, they merely determine where you start."

Believe me, not all of us start in the same place and some people must face huge obstacles before they even get to the starting line.

Several years ago now, my friend Lorne Segal approached me and asked if I would like to lend my powers of persuasion to a good cause that he had been involved with for years. The good cause he had in mind was the Courage to Come Back Awards, an event that he had chaired for the past five years. These annual awards honour individuals who have exhibited great strength, perseverance and resilience in the face of adversity and are an inspiration to their friends, family and community. The awards are also the only fundraiser undertaken by the Coast Mental Health Foundation in support of their programs, which provide much-needed services to a wide range of people within the community. Those services include housing, employment programs, detox and drug treatment, counselling, peer mentoring and even art therapy.

With his incredible powers to persuade, cajole and inspire a diverse range of people in the Vancouver business community to donate their time, talent and money towards something that he is immensely passionate about, Lorne has done an outstanding job of growing this showcase of the power of the human spirit into the premier charity event in Vancouver (regularly sold out to crowds of 900) and to give a face to Coast Mental Health and mental illness.

What Lorne needed from me was simple. He wanted me to pitch for the money during the annual gala event, which for years has been emceed by local broadcast personalities Deborra Hope and Kevin Evans (this year, Global TV news anchor Jill Krop took over for Hope). At the event, each table is provided with pledge forms for guests to write down the amount they would like to donate. Near the beginning of the evening, I come on stage and give a little inspirational talk and then ask everyone to make their pledges. Once the pledge forms have been collected and tallied, I come back on stage (usually after several of the awards have been given out and the audience has met some of the inspiring individuals who benefit from the foundation's programs) to let the audience know how much we've raised and to get them inspired to raise even more. This is a very emotional and exciting part of the evening, as people start to up their donation to see how high we can go. This year, we had almost 1,000 people in attendance and we raised $728,059. Not bad for a night's work (to date the awards have raised more than $4 million for the foundation).

What I get out of the evening is much more profound than anything that I could put into words, for it is impossible to listen to these stories and meet these individuals who have lived through so much, without being moved.

I would like to introduce you briefly to the six recipients of the 2010 Courage to Come Back Awards:

Starr Peardon

Before she found the strength to rebuild her life and redirect her energy to help other troubled women, 58-year-old Starr Peardon was a drug addict and a drug dealer, robbed gas stations and spent her fair share of time behind bars. Following her fifth stint in prison (where she discovered her faith in God) and an eight-week treatment program, Peardon realized that the drugs weren't working for her anymore and she found comfort in helping other women whose lives were as devastated by addiction as her own. Wanting to do more, she eventually convinced the church where she was employed to put up the money to start a recovery house for women. The society that runs the house, which is located in Coquitlam, B.C., has been offering the recovery program for a decade now and has helped as many as 200 women.

Theresa Duggan

Theresa Duggan is a 48-year-old single mother with bipolar disorder. For years, she lived in isolation due to the debilitating nature of her mental illness. So paralyzed by her illness that she didn't brush her teeth for three years, rarely changed her clothes and was in and out of psychiatric wards, it took until her mid-30s for Duggan to receive a diagnosis that was able to determine the proper medication to relieve her of the psychotic episodes that made it impossible for her to function in the real world. Today, she works with Gastown Vocational Services, supporting mentally ill clients. She also does volunteer work and is raising her teenage daughter. She says she shares her story in the hope that it will help others to realize that mental illness is not something you have any control over, it's a chemical imbalance and not something you can simply overcome on your own.

Myrna Cranmer

Today, 59-year-old Myrna Cranmer is an outreach worker with the Downtown Eastside Women's Centre. She travels through the streets of Vancouver's Downtown Eastside seeking out sex-trade workers (women who struggle with poverty, addictions, mental illness and HIV) to offer any support they are willing to accept. Cranmer knows what it is like to live on those very streets. Sent to residential school at the age of five, by any measure she had a difficult life, marked by violence, that culminated in nearly three decades of drug addiction. She spent time in jail for theft, trafficking and assault and was also charged at one point with murder and attempted murder (the charges were later dropped). In 1994, Cranmer woke up one morning and decided she had had enough of life on the streets and dropped in at the Downtown Eastside Women's Centre where she found the information she needed to enter a detox program and then a recovery house. Since turning her life around, she has reconnected with her family and earned a master's degree in anthropology and she is grateful for the opportunity to reach out to other women.

Cindy Thomsen

Up until February 2006, Cindy Thomsen was an average hard-working mom living in Chilliwack, B.C., with her husband and children and employed as a home-support worker. That is, until the morning she woke up feeling so tired and weak that she couldn't pull herself out of bed. After considerable nagging from her husband to go to the hospital, she arrived at Chilliwack General and very shortly afterward fell into a coma. It turned out that Thomsen had contracted an extremely rare form of pneumonia called pneumococcal septicaemia and her body had become septic (her blood had been poisoned by the infection and the virus was attacking every part of her body). Although the doctors pumped her full of antibiotics to fight the virus, there was only a 10 per cent chance that she would make it through the first night. Amazingly, 10 days later, she came out of the coma, but she had suffered significant damage to her body. The bacteria had burned large areas of her face, as well as both of her arms and legs. The only option was to amputate her arms just below the elbow and her legs at mid-calf. Burned parts of her face, including portions of her lips, nose and mouth, also fell off. Not one to give up or give in, Thomsen has learned to walk and use her arms again with the help of prosthetics. She has also had numerous surgeries to reconstruct parts of her face and she bravely faces the world with a "never back down from a challenge" attitude. Thomsen also helps others as a certified peer visitor with the Amputee Coalition of Canada. For her, life is definitely precious.

Mark Ash
In the 1980s, Mark Ash thought of himself as a rock star. Playing in a rock band on some of the biggest stages in

and around Vancouver, his group had a song on the radio and lived the party lifestyle. He had a beautiful wife, two children and a big house. Throughout much of the '90s, he owned and ran the New York Theatre on Commercial Drive in Vancouver. In 2001, his life changed dramatically as the result of a car accident that left him with a serious brain injury, partially paralyzed and unable to talk, walk or take care of himself. Devastated, he lived with his dad for a year and found it difficult to have any hope for the future. On a suggestion from his mental-health team, Ash joined a Canadian Mental Health Association (CMHA) program and moved into a group home where he began to build himself back up one step at a time. He worked on regaining strength in his muscles, relearned to speak both Russian (his first language) and English and listened to music non-stop as a form of therapy to help him through the difficult process. Eventually Ash was able to play guitar once again and he has since formed a band called Reality Check at the CMHA's Pathways Clubhouse in Richmond, B.C. Today, he is independent once more, living in his own place and helping others through a therapy program at GF Strong Rehabilitation Centre and several "Wellness Through Music" programs for brain-injured clients at the Pathways Clubhouse and Vancouver Headway Centre.

Fahreen Mapara

At 10 years old, it's not surprising that Fahreen Mapara enjoys singing in the choir, riding her bike and listening to her iPod. It's also not surprising that her most immediate goal is to be able to master doing the splits. What does distinguish her from other 10-year-olds is the breathing tube attached to her neck 24 hours a day. She was born six weeks premature with a tracheoesophageal fistula, which means that her airway and the tube that the food goes down when she swallows are linked together. As a result, as an infant, whenever she tried to drink milk, she would begin throwing up because everything she swallowed ended up in her lungs. It took four surgeries and a feeding tube in her stomach (that she will need to use for the rest of her life) to allow her to lead a normal life. Although she will never be able to eat and is unable to speak because of damaged vocal cords, she has no difficulty communicating and she is a happy and adventurous child. In addition to enjoying sports such as martial arts, playing the recorder and spending time with friends, Fahreen also volunteers at her school to help new Canadians settle into the community and she is an inspiration to everyone she meets.

The Courage to Come Back Awards celebrate the amazing efforts of real people with real struggles (each one of them living proof that it's never too late to make the most of the life we have) and serves to educate thousands more every year to look squarely into the face of adversity when it's so much easier to look away. As Lorne so eloquently put it at this year's awards ceremony, "These stories would move anyone to tears because they are about the miracles of everyday life. Having witnessed them, we all walk away a little richer than when we walked in, ready to face our own fears and achieve our greatest dreams because by seeing the very best in others — courage, hope, faith, endurance

— we see what we ourselves can become."

You can find out more about the Coast Mental Health Foundation at www.coastmentalhealth.com.

—m—

I turned 68 this past January and I've found that the older you get, the more philosophical you become. So here is a little story that I heard John Maxwell tell on Robert Schuller's *Hour of Power*. The tale explains life, because I know we all have questions about life:

On the first day, God created the dog and said, "Sit all day by the door of your house and bark at anyone who comes by and I'll give you a lifespan of 20 years."

The dog thought about this and then replied, "That's too many years to be barking. Let me keep 10 years and I'll give you the other 10 back."

So God agreed.

On the second day, God created the monkey and said, "Entertain people, do monkey tricks, make them laugh. I'll give you a 20-year lifespan."

The monkey was quick to respond, "How boring. Monkey tricks for 20 years? I don't think so. The dog gave you back 10, so that's what I'll do, too."

"Very well," said God.

On the third day, God created the cow and said, "You must go out in the field with the farmer all day long, suffer under the sun, have calves and give milk to support the farmer. I'm going to give you a lifespan of 60 years."

The cow considered the offer and said, "That's kind of a tough life you want me to live for 60 years. Let me have 20 and I'll give you back the other 40."

So God agreed.

On the fourth day, God created man and said, "Eat, sleep, play, enjoy your life. I'll give you 20 years."

Man looked at God and said, "What, only 20 years? I'll tell you what, I'll take my 20, add the 40 the cow gave you back, the 10 the monkey gave you and the 10 the dog gave you. That makes 80, okay?"

God said, "You've got a deal."

So, that is why for the first 20 years of our lives we eat, sleep, play and enjoy ourselves. For the next 40 years we slave in the sun to support our family. For the 10 years after that, we do monkey tricks to entertain the grandchildren and for the last 10 years we sit on the front porch and bark at everybody that goes by.

That's life!

I like that story because it always reminds me how lucky we are as humans to have such a long lifespan in comparison to many other species. We should make the most of it by pursuing as many dreams as we can. Here's a story about one of mine.

John Furlong, chair of the Vancouver Organizing Committee for the 2010 Olympic and Paralympic Games, sent me a letter in 2006, inviting me to be an ambassador for the Olympics along with 18 other men and women. As he explained it, the ambassadors would be his eyes and ears on the Olympics in communities around B.C., looking for opportunities to engage people around the province and celebrate what is special within each community. In addition to my dream of being emcee for the opening and closing ceremonies, I was excited to be involved in the Olympics any way that I could, so I happily accepted the invitation.

As the Olympics drew near, I got to talking one day to Graham MacLachlan, who is regional president of Olympic partner RBC, and his associate, Tim Manning. This was after all of the people had already been picked for the cross-country Olympic torch run. I asked, "Is there any way you can fit me in to do it?" They said they would keep me in mind. The deadline had already passed, but they gave me the paperwork to fill in and asked that I write a 200-word essay about why I should be chosen. I wrote about my involvement with Variety the Children's Charity and trying to make a difference for the kids. After reading my essay, Graham came to me and said, "You don't want to run with the torch for the regular Olympics, you want to run for the Paralympics in honour of Variety."

I agreed and we moved on to the next step in the vetting process, which was a meeting where I found out everything that would be expected of each torchbearer (when to show up, what to do, etc.). We were also informed that there would be an opportunity to buy the torch after the run for $400.

At the end of the meeting, each torchbearer was given the Paralympic uniform, hat and red mittens.

I was one of 600 bearers of the Paralympic torch to run in a continuous 24-hour relay in downtown Vancouver just prior to the opening ceremonies of the 2010 Paralympics. I found out that I would be running at 7:40 in the morning, so I would have to show up at 5 a.m. My run was to be from Smithe and Howe to Smithe and Burrard streets.

The alarm went off at 3:30 a.m. on Friday, March 12. It was a typical March morning; windy, rainy and cold — I knew it was going to be a day to remember (as it turned out, one of the most emotional days of my life). As I mentioned, my portion of the run was scheduled for 7:40 a.m., but my collection time was 5 a.m. in the downtown core. It was to be a 12-minute, two-block run with the Paralympic torch, which had been lit by the original flame from Mount Olympus in Greece back in October 2009.

Due to the early hour, I thought about sleeping down the hall that night so as not to wake Kay. Shutting off the alarm, I jumped out of bed, had a quick shower and shave and slipped into my pale-blue Paralympic track suit. It was a 50-minute drive to downtown Vancouver with almost no cars on the road, and I had plenty of time to anticipate how the run would go. As I got closer to the collection point, my heart was racing and my palms sweating, which surprised me because I'm not one to be nervous in front of people — ever — but this was different.

I've never really been ill, and do not have any physical disabilities at all, so why be nervous? To be a Paralympian takes so much courage, training and discipline, and I was about to do my small part to honour those athletes who would compete for gold in alpine skiing, biathlon, curling, sledge hockey and other events, representing their countries with honour and pride.

At the collection point, once they checked that I was in my Paralympic tracksuit and had my hat and mittens, they took me downstairs and put me in a little mini bus that went around the circuit, dropping each runner off at their starting spot where they would have their torch lit.

When I was in position and the runner who would light my torch was about 15 seconds away, someone came up to tell me to get ready. It was a surreal moment, as I felt my own anticipation and that of the crowd, almost as if everyone were holding their breath at once.

When some runners got off the bus, they had their family or friends waiting, two or three people there to cheer them on.

I had invited all of my Canada Wide Media staff, my family, children, grandchildren and even the dog, and they were all there when I got to my location. Their support really made it for me.

When the torch runner came up and lit my torch, it was absolutely electrifying as I realized this was the same flame that had travelled all the way from Greece, birthplace of the Olympics.

I didn't actually run my portion of the route. I walked the entire time . . . enjoying every second as cars honked their horns and everyone cheered.

And then it was over, a block away from the Wedgewood Hotel. So we went there for breakfast (all 36 of us).

I was very sad that it had gone so fast. I could have carried it for another hour, it was so exhilarating.

I wasn't the only one in my company who was captivated by the torch. During the Olympic torch run, our VP of sales Debbie McLean ran alongside the torchbearers for three hours. Some were crying. She told me it was the most incredible experience.

What a thrill and what an enormous honour to have been selected to do this, to have the privilege to carry that torch, even if it was only for five or seven minutes. I now have the torch that I carried in my office. After the run, Graham said, "I want to buy the torch for you, for all that you do for the community, as my gift to you."

It was funny too, because the next morning, I was preparing to take the torch back to work to give everyone a chance to see it up close and Kay said to me, "I couldn't find the torch, I was going to clean it for you." Good job she didn't find it because she was going to polish it up not realizing that the blackened marks from the flame are what make it so special.

To have yet another opportunity to be a part of the Olympic experience and to get caught up in the Olympic excitement was quite amazing and something I will always remember.

A week or so after my run, there was a Paralympian lunch sponsored by COLD-FX, where 450 members of the media and associated athletic organizations came together to salute one of the founders of the Paralympic Games, Dr. Robert Steadward, who for 40 years had been pressing the International Olympic Committee for the inclusion of the Paralympic Games with the Olympics. He has, of course, succeeded. Talk about persistence and never giving up on your dream!

Paul Rosen from Thornhill, Ontario, was one of the guest speakers at the lunch. He told us that on June 8, 1999, at the age of 39, his doctors gave him a life expectancy of three months unless he had his entire right leg amputated. He said, "We have to take all the negatives in our lives and turn them into positives. We don't have to settle for mediocrity. If we don't strive to be the best — what's the point?"

Rosen is now 50 and considered the best sledge-hockey player in the world. He said of the Paralympics, "What an honour to play for my country." He is the Canadian team's goalie. They won a gold medal in Turin in 2006 and although they didn't make it to the final in 2010 — his final Paralympic Games — he is still a hero and a role model for anyone with a big dream.

So, it is for the Paul Rosens of this world that I was running, and all the courageous athletes from 50 countries who have turned negatives into positives no matter what, who have not settled for mediocrity and who have persevered and struggled in order to make their dreams come true. They are an inspiration.

How do we turn our negatives into positives? Do we settle for a life of mediocrity or do we strive to be our very best every day? How soon do we give up on our dreams or our goals? Helen Keller once said, "I'd rather be blind, than be born without vision." What is your vision for your family, your business, your country, your life? Ultimately, the decision is yours.

SOMETHING TO THINK ABOUT

In his 1962 book, *Success Unlimited*, Napoleon Hill wrote that you can read the future, anybody's future, by asking them a simple question: "What is your major definite purpose in life — and what plans have you made to attain it?"

According to Hill, 98 out of a hundred will answer, "I haven't any particular aim to make a living . . . and become successful if I can."

You need to count yourself in the two per cent who don't leave everything to chance, by having the courage to make a plan and act on your dreams.

Who were you born to be? How much of your potential have you yet to fulfill? When you look back, do you feel as if you have wasted your opportunities? If you want to make the most of your future, you have to stop feeling like that. Whatever you've done, or not done, it doesn't matter. The question is, what are you going to do next? You have special insights, abilities, talents and gifts. The universe knows this and it wants to help you make the most of them. You can't let age or any other obstacles get in the way of going after what you really want. Dreams don't have to wait.

"Every day, think as you wake up, today I am fortunate to be alive, I have a precious human life, I am not going to waste it. I am going to use all my energies to develop myself, to expand my heart out to others, to achieve enlightenment for the benefit of all beings . . ."
— The Dalai Lama

CHAPTER 9

THERE ARE NOT MANY MISTAKES THAT CANNOT BE RECOVERED FROM

"Our greatest glory is not in never falling, but in rising every time we fall."

— Confucius

Do you know what the following famous people have in common? Francis Ford Coppola, Cyndi Lauper, Walt Disney, Milton Hershey, Dorothy Hamill, Mark Twain and Toni Braxton. Each one of them has filed for bankruptcy at some point in their life.

Francis Ford Coppola: Director of the *Godfather* movie trilogy and winner of five Academy Awards before he was 40 years old, Coppola was $300,000 in debt before the first *Godfather* film was released. After his 1982 musical *One From the Heart* bombed, he filed for bankruptcy. He later got into the wine business and turned his financial situation around.

Cyndi Lauper: Before her big hit song, "Girls Just Wanna Have Fun," was released, Lauper was in a group called Blue Angel. After their record flopped and their manager sued them for $80,000, the band broke up and Lauper was forced into bankruptcy in 1980. She quickly recovered and became an '80s pop icon.

Walt Disney: The man whose name is synonymous with Mickey Mouse and Disneyland, "the happiest place on earth," Disney wasn't always in the black. In 1921, he started a company called Laugh-O-Gram in Kansas City, Missouri, but was forced to file for bankruptcy two years later when his financial backers pulled out. It was that failure that convinced him to head to Hollywood where he became one of the highest-paid animators in history and pursued his big dream, which continues to live on long after his death.

Milton Hershey: Although the company that bears his name was founded in 1903 and continues on today as a very successful business, Hershey experienced his share of failure in life. With only a fourth-grade education, his first career was working as an apprentice printer. He didn't like the business, however, and decided to try his hand at candy-making. His first four business attempts failed and he was forced into bankruptcy before starting his fifth, the Hershey's Food Corporation.

Dorothy Hamill: As the 1976 national, world and Olympic figure-skating champion, Hamill was dubbed America's sweetheart and a doll was made in her likeness. However, after purchasing the struggling Ice Capades, which she tried to revive, she declared bankruptcy. Not one to give up, Hamill continues to be a role model and cheerleader for the sport she loves and she attended the 2010 Winter Olympics as a mentor to the 2008 World Junior Champion, Rachael Flatt.

Mark Twain: Fascinated by inventions that he was sure

would make him rich and successful, Twain (whose real name was Samuel Clemens) lost a fortune, most of it on a printing press that he thought would revolutionize the publishing business. In 1894, he declared bankruptcy and then embarked on an around-the-world lecture tour to pay off his creditors, which he was able to do in full by 1898.

Toni Braxton: Despite selling over 15 million albums in the years leading up to her 1998 filing for bankruptcy, Braxton found herself deep in debt and entangled in a major dispute with her recording company. As a result, all of her household possessions, including several Grammy Awards, were put up for sale. Despite the very public humiliation of going through bankruptcy, Braxton kept her focus on her dream and as a result ended up on Broadway playing Belle in the musical *Beauty and the Beast* (she was the first black woman to star in a Disney musical on Broadway and the first and only black woman to play Belle on Broadway). Since then she has gone on to release four more albums and continue with a very successful singing career.

We all make mistakes in life, sometimes big ones, but we only fail when we give up altogether. If we choose not to give up, our mistakes are simply lessons and signposts along the way to help us figure out what works, what doesn't and where we want to go next.

In his book *It's Your Time*, Joel Osteen talks about how our mistakes can provide us with tremendous opportunities for growth, in the same way that the wind can twist and bend a palm tree to make it stronger. Here's what he says:

"The palm tree was designed to bend, but not break in high winds. A palm tree can bend all the way over until its top touches the ground and still not break.

"Biologists say that during a hurricane, when the palm tree is being bent and pushed over, its root system is actually strengthened by the stress, which gives it new opportunities for growth.

"We all want to be as strong as oak trees, but in these challenging times, we need to bend like the palm tree, and then grow."

I think the biggest mistake we can make in life is to do nothing because then we shut out all opportunity to move forward. Enjoy your mistakes — they're a sure sign that you're learning and growing.

—m—

In the course of my career, my books, speeches and community life, it occurred to me that I was creating a very distinct impression that nothing ever goes wrong in the life of Peter Legge. Of course, considering the business I'm in, it's not surprising that my books and speeches tend to focus on the positive. Everything upbeat, a reflection of endless success, impeccable timing, complete control — never a hint that anything ever goes wrong, or that from time to time there may even be the occasional embarrassing moment.

Let me tell you a story that will help balance the scales. I have told this before in my book *Make Your Life a Masterpiece*, but I think it bears repeating.

At one stage in my life, I sought a career in the United

Kingdom as a comedian. I had had some success making people laugh and figured that with a bit of British luck, I'd go straight to the top.

But in show business, there are always dues to pay. Anyone who has ever made it will tell you stories of dingy dressing rooms, ruthless theatre operators and, worst of all, audiences that eat you alive.

So here I was down in the depths of darkest Wales, doing a circuit of 20 working men's clubs for £6 a night, trying to get blokes who had been down the mine all day to enjoy a few laughs with a beer. I knew nothing about Wales, couldn't pronounce the names of half the towns I was visiting and knew even less of the local lore and legends.

But that didn't seem too important. Humour has universal appeal and on one rainy night in a small Welsh village, right after the singer and the magician, on came Peter.

I went right into my jokes about kids. Hard-driving stories about how rotten they can be, how ungrateful and unnecessary they really are, really funny stuff that had cracked 'em up in London.

Not a laugh. Not even a murmur of a laugh. And 12 minutes later, I gave up, walked off the stage, right into the arms of the furious club owner.

"On your way, mate," he said without further explanation. Clenched mouth, fierce eyes. "Outta town!"

Hurt, puzzled and upset at the lack of response to what I knew was a proven routine, I slunk back to the hotel.

"Aberfan," I said, reading the signs on the stores in the high street. "Aberfan."

And it all clicked and I knew what had gone wrong.

A month before, from high on a hill above the town's small primary school, a tip, the monstrous leftover pile from the diggings in a coalmine, had slipped and raced down the hillside. It slid like a great grey blanket over the school and took the lives of 170 people, most of them children, in the worst disaster of its kind in history.

Many of the working men in the club that night were fathers of those children — still filled with memories of the faces and lives of those young Welsh citizens who had died beneath the Aberfan tip. I felt absolutely awful.

It *is* important to know where you are and to have some knowledge about what's going on. If you don't, as I found out that night, you get exactly what you deserve.

I've never forgotten that Aberfan audience. In a special way, I will share their grief for the rest of my life.

As I mentioned earlier, we all make mistakes and sometimes those mistakes are so big that they seem to define who and what we are. But as the following story proves, as long as we are still alive, we have an opportunity to change our behaviour, choose a different path and maybe even change the world as a result. It is actually two stories with a special connection between them:

Story I
Many years ago, Al Capone virtually owned Chicago. Capone wasn't famous for anything heroic. He was notorious for enmeshing the Windy City in everything from bootlegged booze and prostitution to murder.

Capone had a lawyer who had been nicknamed "Easy Eddie." He was Capone's lawyer for a good reason. Eddie was very good! In fact, Eddie's skill at legal maneuvering kept Big Al out of jail for a long time.

To show his appreciation, Capone paid him very well. Not only was the money big, but Eddie also got special dividends. For instance, he and his family occupied a fenced-in mansion with live-in help and all of the conveniences of the day. The estate was so large that it filled an entire Chicago city block.

Eddie lived the high life, providing his services to Capone and other members of the Chicago Mob, giving little consideration to the atrocities that were committed by the people he defended.

But Easy Eddie did have one soft spot. He had a son whom he dearly loved and Eddie saw to it that his young boy had the best clothes, cars and a good education. When it came to his son, nothing was withheld and price was no object.

Despite his involvement with organized crime, Eddie even tried to teach his son right from wrong. Eddie wanted his son to be a better man than he was.

But even with all of his wealth and influence, there were two important things Eddie couldn't give his son; he couldn't pass on a good name or a good example.

One day, Easy Eddie reached a difficult decision; he made a choice to right the wrongs he had done in the only way that he knew how. He decided he would go to the authorities and tell the truth about Al "Scarface" Capone, clean up his tarnished name and offer his son some semblance of integrity. To do this, he would have to testify against the Mob and he knew that the cost would be great . . . but he testified anyway.

Within the year, Easy Eddie's life ended in a blaze of gunfire on a lonely Chicago street. But in his eyes, Eddie had given his son the greatest gift he had to offer, at the greatest price he could ever pay. Following his death, police removed from his pockets a rosary, a crucifix, a religious medallion and a poem clipped from a magazine.

The poem read:

"The clock of life is wound but once and no man has the power to tell just when the hands will stop, at late or early hour. Now is the only time you own. Live, love, toil with a will. Place no faith in time, for the clock may soon be still."

Story II

The Second World War produced many heroes. One such man was Lieutenant Commander Butch O'Hare. He was a fighter pilot assigned to the aircraft carrier *Lexington* in the South Pacific.

One day his entire squadron was sent on a mission. After he was airborne, he looked at his fuel gauge and realized that someone had forgotten to top up his fuel tank. He would not have enough fuel to complete his mission and get back to his ship.

His flight leader told him to return to the carrier. Reluctantly, he dropped out of formation and headed back to the fleet.

As he was returning to the mother ship, he saw something that turned his blood cold: a squadron of Japanese aircraft was speeding its way toward the American fleet.

With the American fighters gone on a sortie, the fleet

was all but defenceless. He couldn't reach his squadron and bring them back in time to save the fleet, nor could he warn them of the approaching danger. There was only one thing to do. He had to somehow divert the Japanese from the fleet.

Laying aside all thoughts of personal safety, he dove into the formation of Japanese planes. Wing-mounted 50-calibres blazed as he charged in, attacking one surprised enemy plane after another. Butch wove in and out of the now-broken formation and fired at as many planes as possible until all of his ammunition was spent.

Undaunted, he continued with his assault, diving at the planes, trying to clip a wing or tail in the hopes of damaging as many enemy craft as he could, rendering them unfit to fly.

Finally, the exasperated Japanese squadron took off in another direction.

Deeply relieved, Butch O'Hare and his tattered fighter plane limped back to the carrier.

Upon arrival, he reported in and related the events surrounding his return. The film from the gun-camera mounted on his plane told the tale. It showed the extent of Butch's daring attempt to protect his fleet. He had, in fact, destroyed five enemy aircraft.

This took place on February 20, 1942, and for his action Butch became the Navy's first ace of the Second World War and also the first naval aviator to win the Congressional Medal of Honor.

A year later, Butch was killed in aerial combat at the age of 29. His hometown would not allow the memory of this hero to fade and because of that, the O'Hare Airport in Chicago is named in tribute to the courage of this great man.

So the next time you find yourself at O'Hare International, give some thought to visiting Butch's memorial displaying his statue and his Medal of Honor. It's located between Terminals 1 and 2.

So what do these two stories have to do with each other?

Butch O'Hare was Easy Eddie's son.

—m—

Many years ago, I heard a speaker say that virtually everything we know today we learned from someone else. First our parents, our siblings, teachers, professors, mentors, colleagues, schools, universities and the books we read.

For over 20 years, I have committed to read one book a week; 52 books a year. (In 2009, it was 47 books). That's over 1,000 books so far in my life — as I continue to learn from others.

Do you think it's had an impact on my family, values, businesses, communities and work? Absolutely! Charlie "Tremendous" Jones once said, "You will be the same person today in five years except for the people you meet, the places you go and the books you read."

Get out into the world, meet people (and learn all that you can from them), go places (experience as much as you can, you've only got a finite amount of time), and also read up on anything and everything that catches your interest.

—ɯ—

I would like to thank Bryan Locke from Wolf & Co. for sharing the following story:

John is the kind of guy you love to hate. He is always in a good mood, and always has something positive to say. When someone asks him how he's doing, he replies, "If I were any better, I'd be twins!"

He's also a natural motivator. If an employee were having a bad day, John would always be there telling them how to look on the positive side of the situation. His positive outlook on life really made me curious, so one day I went up and asked him about it.

"I don't get it!" I said. "You can't be a positive person all the time. How do you do it?"

"Each morning I wake up and say to myself, you have two choices today," he told me. "You can choose to be in a good mood or . . . you can choose to be in a bad mood. I choose to be in a good mood. Each time something bad happens, I can choose to be a victim or . . . I can choose to learn from it. I choose to learn from it. Every time someone comes to me complaining, I can choose to accept their complaining or . . . I can point out the positive side of life. I choose the positive side of life."

"Yeah, right, it's not that easy," I protested.

"Yes, it is," he said. "Life is all about choices. When you cut away all the junk, every situation is a choice. You choose how you react to situations. You choose how people affect your mood. You choose to be in a good mood or bad mood. The bottom line: it's your choice how you live your life."

I reflected on what he said. Soon after, I left the tower industry to start my own business. We lost touch, but I often thought about him when I made a choice about life instead of reacting to it.

Several years later, I heard that he was involved in a serious accident, falling some 60 feet from a communications tower.

After 18 hours of surgery and weeks of intensive care, he was released from the hospital with rods placed in his back.

I saw him about six months after the accident.

When I asked him how he was, he replied, "If I were any better, I'd be twins. Wanna see my scars?"

I declined to see his wounds, but I did ask him what had gone through his mind as the accident took place.

"The first thing that went through my mind was the well-being of my soon-to-be-born daughter," he replied. "Then, as I lay on the ground, I remembered that I had two choices: I could choose to live or . . . I could choose to die. I chose to live."

"Weren't you scared? Did you lose consciousness?" I asked.

He continued, "The paramedics were great. They kept telling me I was going to be fine. But when they wheeled me into the ER and I saw the expressions on the faces of the doctors and nurses, I got really scared. In their eyes, I read, 'He's a dead man.' I knew I needed to take action."

"What did you do?" I asked.

"Well, there was a big burly nurse shouting questions at me," said John. "She asked if I was allergic to anything. 'Yes,' I replied. The doctors and nurses stopped working as they waited for my reply. I took a deep breath and yelled, 'Gravity!'

"Over their laughter, I told them, 'I am choosing to live. Operate on me as if I am alive, not dead.'"

He lived, thanks to the skill of his doctors, but also because of his amazing attitude. I learned from him that every day we have the choice to live fully.

Attitude, after all, is everything. Therefore, do not worry about tomorrow, tomorrow will worry about itself (each day has enough trouble of its own) and remember, today is the tomorrow you worried about yesterday (and where did that worrying get you?).

Today, as with every day, you have two choices.

I agree with John, that how we respond to the events that happen to us is always a choice. Whether or not we appreciate and make the most of the opportunities and lessons that come our way is more about making an internal decision to do so rather than simply reacting to external circumstances. If you've ever been happy during a stressful time at work or unhappy on a vacation, you understand what I'm talking about here.

It is far better to choose to make the most of whatever is happening at the present in your life than to worry about has already happened . . . otherwise, gravity is sure to get you down.

Here's another of my favourite stories and it illustrates how much our perception affects the way we experience life:

One day, the father of a very wealthy family took his son on a trip to the country for the express purpose of showing him how poor people live. They spent a couple of days and nights on the farm of what would be considered a very poor family.

On their return from their trip, the father asked his son, "How was the trip?"

"It was great, Dad."

"Did you see how poor people live?" the father asked.

"Oh yeah," said the son.

"So, tell me, what did you learn from the trip?" asked the father.

The son answered: "I saw that we have the one dog and they have four. We have a pool that reaches to the middle of our garden and they have a creek that has no end. We have imported lanterns in our garden and they have the stars at night. Our patio reaches to the front yard and they have the whole horizon. We have a small piece of land to live on and they have fields that go beyond sight. We have servants who serve us, but they serve others. We buy our food, but they grow theirs. We have walls around our property to protect us; they have friends to protect them."

The boy's father was speechless.

Then his son added, "Thanks, Dad, for showing me

what true wealth really is."

Isn't perspective a wonderful thing? Makes you wonder what would happen if we all could truly appreciate everything we already have, instead of worrying about what we don't have.

As you may know, Alvin Law and I co-host the annual Variety Telethon every February. Alvin is a remarkable man. He was a thalidomide baby and as a result was born with no arms. He has written a best-selling book called *Alvin's Laws of Life: 5 Steps to Successfully Overcome Anything.*

Based on his considerable accomplishments — he is a talented musician, playing trombone, drums and piano; holds an honours degree in Broadcasting and Communications, is a Certified Speaking Professional (CSP), has won an Emmy Award and raises millions of dollars for charity — Alvin is well qualified to offer advice on how to achieve your dreams. Here are the five principles that underlie Alvin's Laws, which I featured in one of my earlier books:

Attitude is more than just being positive — it's a way of looking at life, ours and everybody else's. It is said to be everything because it is everything. It defines who we are and what we become.

Learning is the greatest gift we give ourselves. It can transform us from nobody into somebody and it is the greatest equalizer on earth. To not learn as much as we can is to disrespect the gift of life. In learning, we must also ask questions. That's good because people need to listen more and talk less. There is knowledge all around us; we just have to listen for the answer. To listen is to learn, and to learn is to grow.

Value your life and spirit. Too many people live another "V," that of victim. It's true, bad things happen to good people, and there are victims. The trouble is there is no answer to the question, "Why me?" Even worse, victims often get stuck in their past when what they need is to live for today and move toward the future. When you focus on moving forward, you never know what you'll discover. Everyone has value — finding it, that's the trick.

Imagination is the key that unlocks the power of potential. It is not owned by the young, but they are best at using it. It defines the difference between obstacles and possibilities. Imagination leads to dreams and dreams make life worth living. Dreams can come true . . . this I know.

Never give up! Easy to say, hard to do. The biggest enemy we will ever encounter is the one we face every time we look in a mirror. Yet mirrors do not reflect who we truly are — our lives do.

SOMETHING TO THINK ABOUT

Do past failures sometimes replay in your mind like a song that you just can't get out of your head?

Do you sometimes wish you could relive a moment, equipped with what you now know and completely change the outcome?

If you answered yes to these questions, congratulations, you're human! We all head down the wrong path from time to time and wind up regretting the choices we've made. But fear and guilt are terribly heavy burdens to carry through life, as is regret.

A lecturer, when explaining stress management to an audience, raised a glass of water and asked, "How heavy is this glass of water?"

Answers called out ranged from 20 grams to 500 grams.

The lecturer replied, "The absolute weight doesn't matter. It depends on how long you try to hold it:

"If I hold it for a minute, that's not a problem.

"If I hold it for an hour, I'll have an ache in my right arm.

"If I hold it for a day, you'll have to call an ambulance.

"In each case, it's the same weight, but the longer I hold it, the heavier it becomes."

He continued: "It's the same way with fear, guilt and regret. If we carry our burdens all the time, sooner or later, as the burden becomes increasingly heavy, we won't be able to carry on. As with the glass of water, you have to put it down for a while and rest before holding it again.

When we're refreshed, we can carry on with the burden."

So, before you return home tonight, put the burden of work down. Don't carry it home. You can pick it up tomorrow. Whatever burdens you're carrying now, let them down for a moment if you can.

Why not take a while to just simply *relax*? Put down anything that may be a burden to you right now and don't pick it up again until after you've rested a while. Life is short. Enjoy it!

Here are some great ways of dealing with the burdens of life:

- Accept that some days you're the pigeon, and some days you're the statue.
- Keep your words soft and sweet, just in case you have to eat them.
- Read stuff that will make you look good if you die in the middle of it.
- Drive carefully. It's not only cars that can be recalled by their maker.
- If you can't be kind, at least have the decency to be vague.
- If you lend someone $20 and never see that person again, it was probably worth it.
- It may be that your sole purpose in life is simply to serve as a warning to others.
- Never buy a car you can't push.
- Never put both feet in your mouth at the same time, because then you won't have a leg to stand on.
- Nobody cares if you can't dance well. Just get up and dance.

THE POWER OF A DREAM

- Since it's the early worm that gets eaten by the bird, sleep late.
- The second mouse gets the cheese.
- When everything's coming your way, realize that you're in the wrong lane.
- You may be only one person in the world, but you may also be the world to one person.
- Some mistakes are too much fun to only make once.
- We could learn a lot from crayons . . . Some are sharp, some are pretty and some are dull. Some have weird names, and all are different colours, but they all have to live in the same box.
- A truly happy person is one who can enjoy the scenery on a detour.

James Joyce once said, "Mistakes are the portals of discovery." It takes patience and a good dose of courage to be able to look for the good in our mistakes, but that is the only way the mistakes of our past can be truly useful to us. So learn from your mistakes, put them in perspective and move on with your life.

As Chris Guillebeau, who is currently on a quest to visit every country in the world, says on his blog, *The Art of Non-Conformity: Unconventional Strategies for Life, Work and Travel*, "the list of really big mistakes that you can't recover from is very short. You can walk into glass doors in Singapore, arrive in Pakistan without a visa, or even double-book yourself on two non-refundable flights from Asia. Most of the time, everything turns out fine."

CHAPTER 10

IT'S NOT THE SIZE OF THE DREAMER, IT'S THE POWER OF THE DREAM

I travelled to London, England, earlier this year for a week of meetings with British magazine publishers and a conference (with over 400 other magazine publishers) for the Periodical Publishers Association of Great Britain. The purpose of my trip was to look for new ideas and tips on how to run my business more effectively.

As I was born in England in 1942, it doesn't take much encouragement for me to take another trip to my homeland and enjoy the opportunity to see some family and friends.

In my book *The Power to Soar Higher*, I told this story of one of my earliest childhood memories in the U.K. Soon after the end of the Second World War, my parents decided to send me to a private school for boys in East Sussex. The school was in a little town called Heathfield, halfway between what is now Royal Tunbridge Wells to the north and the seaside town of Brighton to the south.

I was enrolled at a private school because my parents felt it would afford me more subsequent opportunities than if I were to attend a regular school in London.

It was a big and brave decision for my mother and father. Both were working and the fees they would have to pay would mean huge sacrifices for both of them. But it was one of the first big dreams they had for me. I would begin the next stage of my life with a quality education, coupled with the kind of discipline that is traditionally part and parcel of the highly regulated private school system.

When the train left London's Victoria Station in the winter of 1947, I was just five years old and we were puffing southward into the first big adventure of my young life. I had absolutely no idea what lay before me at Tavistock Hall Preparatory School for Boys in tiny Heathfield.

School uniforms were pretty standard at schools in post-war England, and even today they haven't changed much. We wore short grey pants, knee socks, a grey shirt, striped tie, a maroon blazer and a maroon school cap, complete with the school crest.

With me on the train that morning were other London kids who were headed to the same destination. We sat together for the 90-minute journey and, at the age of five, that 90-minute train trip could well have been a journey halfway around the world.

When I was 12, my parents decided that Canada, and specifically Vancouver, British Columbia, presented infinitely more opportunities for success than did post-war Britain. They were big dreamers, and I would be part of their dream.

The summer before we left for Canada, the annual Tavistock Sports Day was about to take place. Full of vim, vinegar and Olympian dreams, I tried out for every event on the card. But the event in which I really wanted to excel was the Half Mile for Boys. It was the glamour event, the premier race of the day. Four times around the track, the winner invariably ended up being a school hero with adulation of the highest order and at least 15 minutes of fame.

After the time trials, they had a field of 15 — and I hadn't made the cut. I was disappointed, but what the heck, there were other events and I would still have the chance to depart from Tavistock Hall in style. But it was not to be.

Part of the routine at Tavistock Hall required parents to donate trophies for specific Sports Day events. My parents had sent a trophy for, you guessed it, the Boys Half Mile for 12-year-olds and, as you already know, I wasn't, at this stage, in the race!

Enter the head master.

There were 250 of us, all in school uniform, seated for breakfast when he arrived to deliver the news. As always happened when the "head" arrived, the hubbub ceased in an instant. Not a whisper above the sea of porridge bowls.

He fixed me with a stare.

"Legge," he said, "you were too slow to be one of the runners in the half-mile, but your parents have donated a trophy. I guess I'll have to put you in the race."

Incredible motivation for a 12-year-old boy!

So Sports Day came and there I was at the starting line, the 16th runner in a newly augmented field. The gun went off and we ran.

At the end of the first lap, I was dead last, exactly where

I should have been. Then, as I passed the clubhouse turn, I caught the eyes of my mother, father and grandmother and knew that being last in the 1954 Legge Classic would not be good enough for the kid who bore the proud Legge name.

I put my 12-year-old butt — or the English equivalent of the expression — in gear and began to reach out. Bigger steps. Faster steps. An injection of adrenalin to get me going.

At the end of the second lap, I was in 10th place and the family group had now moved to the front of their seats and were cheering me on. At the end of the third lap, I was running fifth and victory seemed entirely possible. My family was standing and cheering wildly.

I won that race. The field dropped away behind me as I plunged victorious into the tape.

How did I win that glorious day all those years ago? I don't know exactly how I did it, but I think that encouragement counted for a lot and, somewhere along the way, self-confidence contributed something as I strove for an attainable goal. Even the headmaster, in his strange way, was throwing out a challenge. I would show him that No. 16 could be No. 1.

I still have the little trophy my mother presented to me on that very special day.

Races aren't always exhausting physical endeavours. They can be as simple as setting a goal that you think may be just beyond your reach, and going for it. You'll be surprised how many times you can take home the prize. It can be big money, power, whatever. It can be as simple as a moment of satisfaction.

I have dreamed many dreams since that day at Tavistock Hall. Some of my dreams — many of them in fact — have come true. And I have always found that races are won lap by solid lap.

I urge you to be there at the starting line for your race, to give it your best every step of the way, and to savour sweet victory when the race is done.

—ᴍ—

When the Vancouver 2010 Winter Olympic Games came to a close on February 28 and the Olympic cauldron was extinguished, millions of Canadians across the country, I am sure, shed a tear with me as 17 unforgettable days came to an end with the closing ceremonies.

Seventeen days, 2,730 athletes, 25,000 volunteers (affectionately referred to as "the smurfs" because of their bright blue jackets) and three billion viewers worldwide, these Olympics Games were a stunning success from every vantage point.

After 17 days, the athletes were no longer separated by flags, they were united by a common dream. The Olympic torch relay was an incredible, absolutely outstanding journey that included the entire country. Did you know that during its journey, the Olympic torch came within an hour's drive of 90 per cent of all Canadians? Vancouver's Big Band leader Dal Richards, 92, told me that carrying the Olympic torch in downtown Vancouver was the most meaningful event in his life.

The greatest triumph over tragedy had to be bronze-medallist figure skater, Joannie Rochette, whose mother died of a sudden heart attack two days before Joannie was to perform her short program skate. It was perhaps one of the bravest performances in Olympic history. In an interview on February 26, on the *NBC Today* program, Rochette explained that she was skating for her mother and also to inspire other athletes, who in training may have fallen 10 times, but must get up and try for the 11th. A lot of people ask, "What is the purpose of the Olympics?" but I think Joannie Rochette has answered that question as succinctly as anyone could. The answer is clear: its purpose is to inspire us to go after our dreams.

There are many amazing young people with inspiring stories.

At the age of 20, Scottish native Fraser Doherty is a seasoned entrepreneur and CEO. He was just 14 when he set up his company SuperJam using his grandmother's secret jam recipes. After cooking jam at home for several years and selling his products at local farmers' markets and to delicatessens, he developed a method of producing jam entirely from fruit and fruit juice that made it healthier and better tasting than regular jams.

After setting up production, creating a brand and perfecting his recipes, Fraser borrowed $9,000 from a bank to produce three flavours: Blueberry & Blackcurrant, Rhubarb & Ginger, and Cranberry & Raspberry, and became the youngest-ever supplier to a major supermarket chain when Waitrose agreed to put his products on their shelves in March 2007. SuperJam now supplies over 1,000 supermarkets in the United Kingdom (including Tesco, Asda Walmart, Morrisons and Waitrose) and is working on expanding overseas.

Today, SuperJam has retail sales of over $1 million a year, is exhibited in the National Museum of Scotland as an "Iconic Scottish Brand" and Fraser was recently named Global Student Entrepreneur of the Year (he is the first-ever winner from outside North America). When the prime minister of the U.K. heard about Fraser's amazing story, he invited him to dinner at Downing Street and commended him on his entrepreneurship.

Fraser's company is also community minded, hosting SuperJam Tea Parties for elderly people who live alone, in care homes or sheltered housing. SuperJam has hosted over 125 events across the U.K. with live music, dancing, scones and SuperJam. Up to 500 guests attend each of these events and they have become a popular outing for elderly people who enjoy the social interaction they provide.

Since launching his company, Fraser has travelled all over the world sharing his story with others. Recently, he visited New York where he spoke to students at Columbia University. From an entrepreneurial point of view, one of the most impressive aspects of his story is that Fraser has retained 100 per cent ownership of his company and the operation is essentially debt-free — success is pretty sweet.

—m—

When he was 12 years old, Craig Kielburger was looking through the weekend newspaper searching for the comics when a headline caught his attention: "Battled child labour, boy, 12, murdered." The story was about a young boy from Pakistan named Iqbal Masih who had been forced into bonded labour in a carpet factory at the age of four. He became an international poster child for the fight against child labour at the age of 10 when he spoke out against the deplorable conditions in which child labourers lived. Many, like Iqbal, were actually chained to the machines they operated to prevent them from running away. They were also starved, beaten and abused. In 1995, Iqbal was brutally murdered as a message to others who would speak out against child slavery.

Shocked and angered by the article, Kielburger knew he had to do something to help. After doing some research to learn more, he took the article to school and shared it with a group of Grade 7 classmates and together, they decided to form a group called (Kids Can) Free the Children.

Later that same year, Kielburger travelled to Asia at the invitation of a family friend from Bangladesh to see for himself the conditions in which the children were being forced to work. During his stay, he found out that Prime Minister Jean Chrétien was also travelling in India. He asked to meet with the prime minister to talk about child labour issues but was denied. Not willing to leave it at that, Kielburger arranged a press conference and announced that the prime minister had a moral responsibility to take action on child labour. Eventually, Mr. Chrétien agreed to meet with him and as a result, brought up the issue of child labour with both the president of Pakistan and the prime minister of India during his time in Asia.

It wasn't long before Free the Children began to receive international attention and today, the organization is the world's largest network of children helping other children through education, with more than one million youth involved in innovative education and development programs. To date, Free the Children has built over 500 schools and organized projects in 45 developing countries. On average, 65 per cent of the organization's annual funding comes from funds raised by young people.

Building on the success of Free the Children, Kielburger and his brother Marc founded Me to We, a social enterprise organization that donates half of its annual profits to Free the Children by selling products such as organic fair-trade clothing and hosting educational trips to developing countries. The aim of Me to We is to eventually cover all of Free the Children's administrative costs, so all donations to the charity can go directly to projects. The organization reinvests the other half to grow the social enterprise and promote the ideals of volunteerism, service to others and social involvement.

—ɯ—

It was through Me to We that my friend Lorne Segal became acquainted with the Kielburgers and was subsequently inspired with a dream of his own that resulted in an amazing event called We Day debuting in Vancouver last fall.

A few years ago, Lorne had been invited to a conference called Connecting for Change where he had the opportunity to chat with Roxanne Joyal (Roxanne is married to Marc Kielburger). Shortly after their meeting, Lorne arrived at his office to find a handmade basket with hand-beaded necklaces (the same kind that are worn by the Masai Mara warriors) and an invitation for him to join Craig and Marc Kielburger on a Me to We trip to Kenya. Realizing that this was an incredible opportunity for his children, Chanelle and Matthew, to experience first-hand how young people have the power to engage in making the world a better place, Lorne decided that it would be a family trip.

It was a transformational journey. While in Africa, Lorne and his family helped to build a school, worked on a clean water project and visited villages where they witnessed the realities of poverty. Returning to Canada, they were so excited about the potential of Me to We to grow local awareness and involvement that Lorne began discussions with the Kielburger brothers about the possibility of a Vancouver We Day, essentially a rock concert for social change that would celebrate the power of young people to change the lives of others and feature some of the world's top social-issues speakers and entertainers.

During the next two years, Lorne galvanized support within the Vancouver business community to allow 16,000 young people to attend the event free of charge at the same time that Chanelle and Matthew became ambassadors for We Day, hosting events at both of their schools and giving presentations to local school superintendents, the minister of education and even the Vancouver Board of Trade.

On September 29, 2009, Vancouver's GM Place stadium was filled with 16,000 student leaders from across the region, in turn listening intently and cheering enthusiastically for an inspirational lineup of speakers and entertainers including the Dalai Lama, Governor General Michaelle Jean, the Canadian Tenors, Mia Farrow, Sarah McLachlan, Jane Goodall, the cast of *Degrassi: The Next Generation*, former child soldier Michel Chikwanine and singer Jason Mraz.

It's amazing how one person's dream can inspire others to take action on a dream of their own and in this case, the dream of one child has influenced the hopes and dreams of an entire generation to make the world a better place.

—∿—

Australian teenager Jessica Watson is another young person with a big dream and the determination to make it happen. Earlier this year, Jessica returned from a seven-month voyage that has made her, arguably, the youngest person to sail solo (non-stop) around the world. According to the rules set out by the International Sailing Federation World Sailing Speed Record Council, no other person was allowed to give her anything during the journey and she could not moor to any port or other boat. She was also required to pass the four capes (Cape Horn, Cape Agulhas, Cape Leeuwin and the Cape of S.E. Tasmania) and cross the equator (which she did on November 19, 2009) at some point during her voyage.

Imagine being 16 years old and alone at sea for seven months, relying only on your own wits. The route she set for herself took Jessica through some of the world's most treacherous waters and she battled through huge storms along the way, enduring waves as big as 12 metres tall that knocked her boat on its side seven times. During the journey she also had to do more than a few repairs to the boat and her equipment, including repairs to the engine's fuel pump, the mainsail, the wind generator, the toilet, the stove and the battery monitor.

As she sailed into Sydney Harbour at the end of her trip, tens of thousands of people came out to welcome her home after a 23,000-nautical-mile journey that she described as being incredibly lonely. Prior to her voyage, Jessica had not sailed on her own and during a trial run for her solo journey she accidentally crashed into a freighter (which led to quite a bit of criticism about her being too young and inexperienced to undertake such a trip). In an interview with the *Los Angeles Times*, she explained her reason for taking on the challenge. "I wanted to challenge myself and achieve something to be proud of," she said. "And yes, I wanted to inspire people. I hate being judged by other people's expectations of what a 'little girl' is capable of. It's no longer just my dream or voyage. Every milestone out here isn't just my achievement, but an achievement for everyone who has put so much time and effort into helping getting me here."

Amazingly, at the end of her journey, Jessica Watson told the crowd, "I don't consider myself a hero, I'm an ordinary girl. You don't have to be someone special to achieve something amazing, you've just got to have a dream, believe in it and work hard. I'd like to think I've proved that anything really is possible if you set your mind to it."

Wise words.

As each one of these young people proves, it isn't the size of the dreamer, it's the power of the dream that really counts. Dreams have the power to shape our lives and inspire us to do more and be more. There are moments in all of our lives that we remember better than all of the others because they were the ones that triggered some mechanism within us that set us off in a new direction, the right direction . . . the way that we just knew we were meant to be going.

—⫘—

Here are some thoughts and tips that I have collected over the years to help you get moving in the direction of your own dreams.

Believe in yourself

What you think of yourself and your abilities, more than anything else, will determine your future. As Henry Ford said, "Those who think they can and those who think they can't are both right!" Which one will you be?

Identify and acquire your most-needed skills

Ask yourself this question, "What three skills, if I developed them to my fullest potential, would help me the most in achieving my dream?" Once you have identified what they are, don't waste any time. I guarantee you that developing those skills will change your life.

Seek out a mentor

One of the most important things you can do is to develop a relationship with someone you respect and admire. A mentor can be a source of knowledge, wisdom, advice, friendship and encouragement — as someone who has already been there, done that, a mentor can help to keep you on track and heading in the right direction.

Focus on your priorities

If you don't know what your priorities should be, ask yourself this, "What is the most valuable use of my time?" Focus on the important work that will get you closer to your dream.

Create your own mission statement

Sonja Bata of Bata Shoes, the footwear empire that spans the globe, has a simple and powerful mission statement: To

Shoe the World. In their book, *Built to Last*, authors James Collins and Jerry Porras advise that a mission statement needs to be clear, compelling and have what they call a "big, hairy, audacious goal" that serves as a unifying focal point. "So what is your big, hairy, audacious goal?"

Do your homework
Take time to think through your plans. Work out the steps that it will take to realize your dream and consider all of the ways it will affect your life and the sacrifices you will need to make to get there. Committing to do the homework required to make your dream a reality is the first real step on the road to success.

Build your own network of contacts
Actively search out people whose expertise meshes with your own interests and goals and network with them. Many organizations and interest groups have regular meetings — find the ones that can help you fulfill your dream.

Develop your people skills
People skills constitute 85 per cent of your success in life, while technical skills account for just 15 per cent. The quality of interpersonal relationships between you and the people who can help you achieve your dream will directly affect your level of success. There are numerous courses and programs that can teach you about empathy, negotiation, conflict resolution, communicating with tact and many other interpersonal skills.

Have some chutzpah

One trait that is common to many successful people is good old-fashioned moxie — the kind of irresistible force of character, energy, ingenuity and audacity that makes people memorable. Don't take no for an answer, show some initiative, take a different tack and work your way to yes. Show people that you are passionate about your goals and dreams.

Take responsibility for your own actions

Don't blame others when things go wrong; you can't control the behaviour of others. Look in the mirror. If something is not working, it is up to you to fix it —and then get moving again.

Feel the fear and do it anyway

Mark Twain said, "Courage is resistance to fear, mastery of fear, not absence of fear." Make a habit of doing the things you fear. Pushing through your fear and mustering the courage to face challenges is critical to all of your successes. As Eleanor Roosevelt said, "You gain strength, courage and confidence by every experience in which you really stop to look fear in the face. You are able to say to yourself, 'I have lived through this horror. I can take the next thing that comes along.' You must do the thing you think you cannot do."

Learn the importance of the word "how"

When faced with a challenge, release your creative juices and let them flow. Don't worry about the "what" or the "why," just ask yourself "how." Creative problem-solving is one of the cornerstones of success in any endeavour.

Know that life is unfair — then get over it
Things are not always going to go your way. That's life. Accept it and remember that while problems are challenging, they also provide an opportunity for you to grow and become more resilient. Rise to the challenge of adversity and keep pushing on. Sir Winston Churchill said, "Never, never, never, never give in."

Set aside time to problem-solve
Take half an hour a day to gaze out the window and think about any challenges you may be facing. The best decisions are the ones made when you take the time to think things through.

Explore the world
Travel and life experiences enrich our lives and enhance our understanding of others. The richer your life experience, the greater your success will be.

Commit to lifelong learning
Invest some time and money in continuing your education. Take courses, attend seminars or workshops, seek out new interests and ideas. The future belongs to those who continue to learn and develop their minds. In his 87th year, the remarkable artist and inventor Michelangelo said, "And yet I am still learning."

Help yourself take action

Ask yourself the following questions. The answers will provide you with the ideal starting point for launching your dream.

- Where am I now and how did I get here?
- Where am I going and why do I want to go there?
- What are the obstacles and what am I going to do about them?

Start today

There's no perfect time to start working towards your dream, so why not take that first step right now? As Dr. Seuss so eloquently put it, "Congratulations! Today is your day. You're off to great places! You're off and away! Your mountain is waiting. So, get on your way."

SOMETHING TO THINK ABOUT

The following was taken from a sign on the wall of Shishu Bhavan, the children's home in Calcutta supported by Mother Teresa:

People are unreasonable, illogical and self-centered
LOVE THEM ANYWAY
If you do good, people will accuse you of selfish, ulterior motives
DO GOOD ANYWAY
If you are successful, you will win false friends and true enemies
SUCCEED ANYWAY
The good you do will be forgotten tomorrow

DO IT ANYWAY
Honesty and frankness make you vulnerable
BE HONEST AND FRANK ANYWAY
What you spend years building may be destroyed overnight
BUILD ANYWAY
People really need help but may attack you if you help them
HELP PEOPLE ANYWAY
Give the world the best you have and you'll get kicked in the teeth
GIVE THE WORLD THE BEST YOU'VE GOT
ANYWAY

Mother Teresa dedicated her life to helping others without any expectations about what she would receive in return. It's not a bad philosophy for the rest of us as we pursue our many dreams. Take these eight principles and apply them to your life, your career, your family and your community and you will discover that this wisdom will move you from success to significance.

AFTERWORD

POWER UP YOUR DREAMS

When I started out in my career, I had no titles. But then I didn't start out seeking titles, money, recognition, etc. I started out with hopes and dreams.

I think that titles, money and awards are a nice by-product of success, but of and by themselves they are not enough to make life worthwhile. The industry that I'm in and my chosen field as a speaker, is hardly a career to be hidden. But awards alone are not enough to motivate someone for the amount of time it takes to be successful.

What has always inspired me is my many dreams and even though I may have fulfilled some of the biggest ones, I still have plenty more:

- I want to stay healthy.
- I want to stay married.
- I want to continue growing my reputation.
- I want a strong relationship with my children and my grandchildren.
- I want to build my company and eventually pass it on to my daughters if they are interested.
- I want to do as much as I can for the community.
- I want to continue speaking (realizing that my runway of life is getting shorter).
- I want to have a retirement property in the sun somewhere where Kay and I can play golf and have

the whole family join us for vacations and special celebrations.
- I want to keep reading and learning and . . .

What other dreams do you have?

What are you doing to achieve those dreams?

Vancouver's Empire Stadium was torn down in the spring of 1993, something that often happens to old stadiums. With it went a lot of rubble and even more memories.

The new Empire Field, built for the 2010-2011 Canadian Football League season, opened on June 20, 2010, on the very same site.

My father was in that old stadium on a hot August 7 in 1954, when history was made. Along with some 30,000-plus spectators, Dad witnessed the race between England's Roger Bannister and Australian runner John Landy. For the first time in history, two athletes ran a mile in less than four minutes in the same race. Everest had been conquered the year before and now another "impossible" barrier had come down, another dream of mankind would go into the record books.

Coming into Vancouver for the then British Empire Games, both Bannister and Landy were already sub-four-minute milers. Bannister was the world's first, at 3:59.4 in England. Six weeks later in Turku, Finland, Landy did it in 3:58.0.

The world was waiting for a battle of the champions in Vancouver. Who would win? Could Landy beat Bannister?

For many months, Bannister had trained hard in England, setting his sights on a mile in less than four minutes. Regularly, his long-time Oxford friend Chris Chataway paced him, offering him not just challenge, but the inspirational words that might help him change the record books forever.

Despite the "first-person-under-four-minutes" fame that followed his assault on the clock in England, Bannister arrived in Vancouver full of doubt. After attaining the impossible, he now needed a miracle. To win, to beat Landy, must have seemed like a goal beyond comprehension — not helped by many on the sidelines who were saying he could never do it. It would be interesting to know, even at this late date, how many of Bannister's family, friends, coaches and athletic peers really believed then that the race and the time might be his. Four times round the brand new Empire Stadium track in less than four minutes — and beat the Australian doing it! The tallest of orders.

For many years, a life-size statue of the record-breaking race's most compelling moment stood outside Empire Stadium. It showed Landy in the lead during the last 150 yards. The drama and the irony was that he was looking over his left shoulder as he ran, the precise moment when Bannister streaked by him on his right and went on to victory. Bannister's time was 3:58.8 and Landy's was 3:59.6. They called it the Miracle Mile.

I have often wondered how Roger Bannister — now Sir Roger, and a teacher at Oxford — kept his dream alive when so many must have fed his mind with the distinct possibility of failure. What an enormous ability to focus so clearly on one magnificent goal.

It's vital for all of us to patiently nurture our dreams.

I'm not talking about instant results that can be measured with yardsticks, but Big Dreams. Doggedly driving yourself to achieve the things you want, the things that you have identified as being important to you. In this instant world, where results must happen right now, too many people become discouraged, impatient, depressed, downcast and disheartened. Too many give up too soon. They walk (or run) away from their dreams, cop out on life's big opportunities that deliver only when there is persistence, a will to stick with it, to know that records, even Landy's record, can be licked.

Each of us must have goals and dreams in our professional life, personal life and spiritual life. We must go after our dreams with the same earnestness, intensity and gusto as Sir Roger Bannister and John Landy once did.

SOMETHING TO THINK ABOUT

Have you been waiting for the right time to reach for your dreams? Have you been waiting for the right circumstances? Perhaps you've been waiting for the right opportunity to go after your dreams?

My, you are patient, aren't you?

You could be waiting forever, you know. Time is an illusion. Circumstances are what you make them. Opportunity is a whisper that waits for your invitation; it doesn't burst in and shout its arrival. Now is the right time. Circumstances change when you take action. Opportunity is yours for the making. So what are you really waiting for?

Value every minute, every day — time waits for no one. It's time to power up your dreams.

Lance Bowerbank of Westcoast Moulding & Millwork Limited recently sent me this updated version of a story that you may have seen before. It's worth keeping in mind as you consider when and how you are going to implement the important dreams in your life:

Imagine that you have won the following prize in a contest: each morning your bank will deposit $86,400 in your private bank account for your own personal use. However, this prize has rules, just as any game undoubtedly has certain rules.

Here is the first set of rules:

1. Everything that you don't spend during each day will be taken away from you.
2. You may not simply transfer money into some other account. You may only spend it. Each morning upon awakening, the bank opens your account with another $86,400 for that day.

This is the second set of rules:

1. The bank can end the game without warning; at any time it can say, "It's over, the game is over!"
2. The bank can close the account in an instant and you will not receive a new one.

What would you personally do? Most likely, you would buy anything and everything you wanted, right? Not only for yourself, but for all the people in your life. Maybe even for people you don't know, because you couldn't possibly spend it all on yourself and the people in your life, right? You would try to spend every single cent, and use it all up every day, right?

Actually, this game is a reality, but not with money!

Each of us is in possession of such a magical bank. We just don't always realize that is what it is.

The magical bank is time.

Each morning we awaken and receive 86,400 seconds as a gift of life, and when the day is done, any remaining time is gone and not credited to us. What we haven't lived up to that day is lost forever. Yesterday is forever gone.

Each morning the account is refilled, but the magical bank can dissolve our account at any time . . . without warning.

So, what will you do with your 86,400 seconds? Think about that and always remember this: enjoy every second of your life, because time races by so much quicker than we think. Take good care of yourself and savour the life you have. Live each day to the fullest, be kind to one another and be forgiving. Harbour a positive attitude and always be the first to smile.

Here's wishing you a wonderful, beautiful 86,400 seconds, each and every day. Now go and live your dream!

ACKNOWLEDGEMENTS

The Power of a Dream is, of course, about having dreams in life — and making them happen. One of my own dreams has been to share all that I've learned from my own experiences with the rest of the world, both through my speaking engagements and my writing.

This is now the 14th book that I've published, and I'm so grateful to have had the opportunity to continue sharing my stories with thousands of readers over the years, and helping them to gain new perspectives on their own lives.

I am also thankful to have a supportive team behind me, without whom this book would have not been possible:

Tashon Ziara — My talented writer, editor and researcher, whose remarkable word craft has brought my stories and ideas to vivid life.

Kim Mah — Our sharp-eyed editor, who works to polish each sentence to perfection.

Cathy Mullaly — Our imaginative art director, who designed the dust jacket with a meticulous eye.

Ina Bowerbank — Our hardworking typographer, who patiently laid out these pages without missing a single detail.

Heidi Christie — My dedicated personal assistant, who keeps me organized throughout my most challenging days.

And my special thanks go to Dr. Terry Paulson, Ph.D, for inspiring this book's subtitle, *Your Dream is Still Possible*.

I hope you enjoy reading this book, as much as I enjoyed putting it together for you.

— Peter Legge, O.B.C.

ABOUT THE AUTHOR

Dr. Peter Legge, OBC • L.L.D. (Hon) • D.Tech (Hon)
• CSP • CPAE • HoF

Peter Legge is Chairman and CEO of Canada Wide Media Limited, the largest independently owned publishing company in Western Canada, controlling a network of over 50 magazines across the country with over $30 million in sales annually.

In addition, Peter travels the world as a motivational speaker, accepting more than 100 assignments each year from clients who know that when he speaks, his words will be a catalyst for positive change. He has received the prestigious Golden Gavel Award from Toastmasters International and was voted "Top Speaker in North America," in company with Dr. Robert Schuller and Stephen Covey. Peter has also been inducted into the Speakers Hall of Fame by both the National Speakers Association in the United States and the Canadian Association of Professional Speakers.

Peter is tireless in his commitments to many worthwhile organizations. As co-host of the annual Variety — The Children's Charity Telethon for over 30 consecutive years, he has assisted in raising more than $130 million for the charity. He is also an International Ambassador for Variety International.

His efforts have not gone unnoticed. Among his many honours, Peter has received the Golden Heart Award from The Variety Club and has been invested into the Venerable

Order of St. John of Jerusalem, where he has now been promoted to Commander.

He has been awarded the Order of the Red Cross and named Citizen of the Year for his commitment to the community. He has been honoured with Honorary Doctor of Laws degrees from Simon Fraser University, Royal Roads University and the BC Institute of Technology, and he is a past Chair of the Vancouver Board of Trade.

He is the recipient of the Nido Qubein Philanthropy Award presented to him at the NSA Convention in Atlanta in July 2005.

In 2006, he was appointed one of 18 ambassadors to the Vancouver 2010 Olympic and Paralympic Winter Games. In the same year, Sales and Marketing Executives International awarded Peter with the Ambassador of Free Enterprise in Dallas, Texas.

In 2009, Peter was invested into the Order of British Columbia, the highest civilian honour that the province can award.

Peter is also the author of 13 previous books that have inspired thousands of readers the world over with their powerful motivating messages. In all that he has achieved, Peter attributes his success to four factors: persistence, patience, a positive attitude and passion.

To contact Peter Legge, write to:
Peter Legge Management Company Ltd.
4180 Lougheed Highway, 4th Floor
Burnaby, BC V5C 6A7 Canada
Telephone: 604-299-7311

Email: plegge@canadawide.com
Website: www.peterlegge.com

To book Peter to speak at your next convention, AGM
or association meeting, contact:
Heidi Christie, Manager of Speaker Services,
Peter Legge Management Company Ltd.,
at 604-473-0332 or hchristie@canadawide.com

To order Peter's books, CDs and other products, please
contact Heidi Christie at the address above.